Lean Blockchain Systems Thinking

Lean Thinking has its roots in ideas developed for process improvement in the 1900s. Systems Thinking was discussed as far back as the 1950s. Blockchain technology is based on work that started in the 1990s and was implemented soon after Satoshi Nakamoto published his Bitcoin whitepaper in 2009. Together, these three components—Lean, Blockchain, and Systems Thinking—provide a revolutionary force in process management efficiency and effectiveness.

This book provides a perspective on the advantages of blockchain technology that is rarely covered in business books as well as specialist blockchain-related content. The focus has been the use of Cryptocurrencies as a store of financial value and as an instrument of speculation, like the stock market. This book shows that blockchain, together with Lean and Systems Thinking can provide multiple advantages for societies and the environment. It can be used effectively to meet sustainable development goals (SDGs).

Readers will appreciate that blockchain within Lean practices and Systems Thinking opens opportunities for fundamental organizational transformation, improved strategic decision-making, increased interoperability, and a fairer, more sustainable, and less wasteful world. This book clarifies how the integration of blockchain technology as an organizational concept integrates Lean principles and Systems Thinking. This brings a transformative shift in process design, increasing productivity while minimizing waste across sectors such as industry, public services, governance, supply chains, and social frameworks.

Lean Blockchain Systems Thinking

Reinventing Value Streams

John Dennis and Machiel Tesser

A PRODUCTIVITY PRESS BOOK

Designed cover image: T&F

First published 2025
by Routledge
605 Third Avenue, New York, NY 10158

and by Routledge
4 Park Square, Milton Park, Abingdon, Oxon, OX14 4RN

Routledge is an imprint of the Taylor & Francis Group, an informa business

ISBN: 9781032986333 (hbk)
ISBN: 9781032986326 (pbk)
ISBN: 9781003599715 (ebk)

DOI: 10.4324/9781003599715

Typeset in Garamond
by Deanta Global Publishing Services, Chennai, India

Dedication

I am eternally grateful for the love and unwavering support of my Mam and Dad, Audrey and Norman. Without their encouragement and belief in me, none of this journey would have been possible. Their guidance and strength have been the cornerstone of my achievements.

John Dennis, June 2024

Gratitude

Thank you to everyone who has contributed to the conversation and provided feedback and insights. Your support and encouragement have been invaluable.

Contents

Preface

Vulnerabilities and inefficiencies in traditional business models, supply chains, financial systems, and government processes are increasingly being exposed.

There is an underlying chronic waste and variation in our supply chains, business transactions, and government processes. Over-production, excessive inventories, delays, corruption, pollution, and market uncertainty are just some of the negative outcomes.

These challenges emphasize the importance of creating more sustainable and adaptable systems.

We look forward to a brighter future with the seamless integration of supply chains, trade finance, and logistics with efficient and waste-free flow of goods, services, data, and payments (Chapter 2: Purpose).

This transformation will be driven by improved policies and procedures (the human element) (Chapter 5: Principles, Chapter 7: Procedures) as well as the digitalization of services, production, and supply chains, enhanced by the connectivity between machines and systems, and the adoption of advanced process control techniques such as digital twins (Chapter 1: Innovation, Chapter 9: Tokenization, Chapter 6: Building Blocks).

Use of blockchain to facilitate trusted transactions reduces the reliance on intermediaries, leading to cost savings and reduction in waiting times.

Blockchain is becoming a fundamental pillar of Industry 4.0 and a transformation tool in Supply Chain Management. Blockchain, together with Lean and Systems Thinking, will enable the creation of fully automated and autonomous supply chains (ASC) that share real-time data and enhance the transparency of business operations (Chapter 8: Kanban).

The resulting improvements will greatly enhance collaboration, reduce waste, increase sustainability, and improve balance across different silos, stakeholders, and industries (Chapter 3: Balancing).

To move to this next level of efficiency and sustainability, we must first recognize the faults and negative outcomes of our current traditional and centralized systems (Chapter 4: Cause and Effect) and follow a logical path and scientific framework for improvement (Chapter 10: DMAIC).

We hope this book will help with the understanding of Lean, Blockchain technology, and Systems Thinking, which combined can be a transformational force for good in both business and society.

About the Authors

John Dennis is Master Black Belt in Lean Six Sigma and the founder of Blockchain SVCS Ltd., UK. He is also the current Chairman of the International Lean Six Sigma Institute. John is Seasoned Practitioner, Facilitator, Coach, and Trainer of Process Improvement, Quality Control, Lean Management, and Project Management in Manufacturing, Services, and Information Systems environments.

He has worked with Senior Operations Managers and Executives in Capability Transfer via coaching and mentoring to educate them in the application of Lean and Six Sigma methodology. Clients have recently included NHS, UBS Bank, STAAR Surgical Group, Hoffman La Roche, Zimmer Biomet, Ferrexpo Mining, Novartis, Croda Chemicals, The Welding Institute (TWI Cambridge UK), Morrison Data Services, Gates Engineering, PD Ports, and State Farm Insurance.

John gained his experience in Lean Six Sigma process improvement while working for Instrument Control Services (GE Automation), Entergy Systems, and as Senior Project Manager for IBM Global Services in the USA. John has been a PMP with the Project Management Institute since 2000. He graduated from Loughborough University in Physics, and York University in Education, and also has an MBA from the University of New Orleans.

Machiel Tesser is a pioneer in the blockchain and Lean System Thinking communities in the Netherlands. He has been an advocate for integrating Blockchain technology into lean process improvement and system design for several years. His work emphasizes the use of blockchain in creating an "Economy of Things," where connected devices and agents can autonomously interact and transact, driven by technologies like IoT and AI.

Introduction

Why Lean + Blockchain + Systems Thinking?

"Lean thinking" has its roots in ideas developed for process improvement in the 1900s.[1] "Systems Thinking" was discussed as far back as the 1950s.[2] "Blockchain" technology is based on work that started in the 1990s[3] and was implemented soon after Satoshi Nakamoto published his Bitcoin whitepaper[4] in 2009.

Together, these three components, Lean + Blockchain + Systems Thinking, provide a revolutionary force in process management efficiency and effectiveness.

Lean

"Lean" is the name given to a framework of principles and tools used for optimizing processes through continuous problem-solving and improvements, involving all levels and categories of stakeholders and across the full value-stream. This results in reduced waste and improved flow of value. In this book, we will use the symbol shown in Figure 0.1 when we discuss concepts that are derived from Lean principles:

Figure 0.1 Symbol used when discussing Lean principles.

Blockchain

Blockchain technology facilitates an improved framework for organizational structures, business strategies (that benefit the many rather than the few), and fairer and more effective incentive mechanisms. Blockchain removes non-value-added intermediaries and silos of information by providing one data platform that can be trusted by all stakeholders.

In this book, we will use the fingerprint symbol as shown in Figure 0.2 when we are discussing concepts that are derived from Blockchain technology:

Figure 0.2 Symbol used when discussing Blockchain principles.

Systems Thinking

Systems Thinking is the concept of focusing on the goals and outcomes of the whole system, including society, the earth, suppliers, producers, and end-users instead of the goals of the individual stakeholders or the component parts of the system.[5] Systems Thinking looks for balance, collaboration, and cooperation between the component parts of systems, which results in better and more sustainable outcomes for all stakeholders. Systems Thinking requires that we break down barriers between organizational units and remove silos of information by providing greater interoperability.[6]

In this book, we will use the "thinking head" symbol as shown in Figure 0.3 when we are discussing concepts that are derived from Systems Thinking:

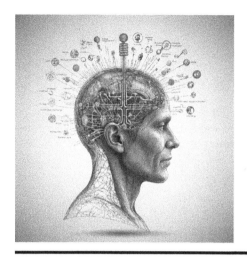

Figure 0.3 Symbol used when discussing Systems Thinking principles.

This book clarifies how the integration of Blockchain technology as an organizational concept incorporates Lean principles and Systems Thinking. This will bring a transformative shift in process design, increasing productivity while minimizing waste across sectors such as industry, public services, governance, supply chains, and social frameworks.

5× Why Should I Read This Book?

Why #1: Organizational Revolution

Blockchain facilitates a unique way of organizing processes, which aligns with the core principles of Lean and Systems Thinking. By leveraging peer-to-peer value flows, organizations can redesign their architectures, facilitating Lean's goals of continuous improvement, waste reduction, and optimized flow of value. In addition, it can meet the goals of Systems Thinking, benefiting the wider community of all stakeholders and achieving fairer and more sustainable outcomes.

Why #2: Strategic Decision-Making

Blockchain offers a paradigm shift in how businesses operate. Understanding its potential impact is crucial for making strategic decisions. Organizations must determine whether to focus solely on optimizing existing processes or embrace blockchain as a game-changer. Like the transformative impact of the internet, blockchain's potential to revolutionize interactions and value exchange is profound.

Why #3: Simplified Explanation and Education

Training and education can demystify blockchain's concepts and potential applications. Blockchain is 90% a process redesign challenge and 10% a technology challenge. By providing training with clear explanations and examples, it is easier to understand how your processes can be redesigned to best leverage the power of decentralization, collaboration, consensus, immutability, and provenance.

Why #4: Strategic Advisory and Adaptation

Just as overlooking the internet's disruptive potential led to poor decision-making in the past, neglecting blockchain today could result in being left behind and obsolete. Lean consultants must recognize the transformative potential of blockchain and its Systems Thinking approach and incorporate it into their recommendations. Failing to do so could hinder an organization's ability to streamline processes and stay competitive in evolving industries.

BLOCKCHAIN ISHIKAWA

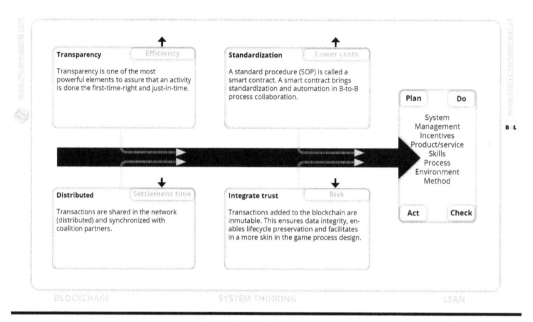

Figure 0.4   The 4 categories of inputs which are necessary to be controlled for efficient and effective management of processes and systems. As suggest by Machiel Tesser 2020.

Why #5: Integration with Lean Principles

Blockchain's decentralized nature and the removal of the need for trusted intermediaries align with Lean's focus on eliminating bottlenecks and waste. Integrating blockchain requires adapting Lean principles and concepts as a guide through the transition.

Consultants and process designers play a pivotal role in ensuring that blockchain adoption complements Lean's ethos of continuous improvement and sustainable processes.

In summary, by embracing blockchain within Lean practices and Systems Thinking, we open opportunities for fundamental organizational transformation, improved strategic decision-making, increased interoperability, and a fairer, more sustainable, and less wasteful world.

Just as the internet has revolutionized business processes over the past 35 years, blockchain's potential impact for the next 35 years is substantial and deserves proactive exploration and adoption.

Notes

1. Fredrick Taylor's scientific management was highly influential on lean manufacturing. https://bobemiliani.com/what-is-lean-management/
2. Systems Thinking was launched by Ludwig von Bertalanffy and others in the 1950s as an interdisciplinary movement with a broad and bold scientific program. https://academic.oup.com/edited-volume/27968
3. In 1991, Stuart Haber and W. Scott Stornetta released a research paper titled "How to time-stamp a digital document". The research paper discussed the immutability of digital records with a Time Stamping Service (TSS) that uses hash functions and digital signatures to verify the originality of a specific document. https://immutablerecord.com/the-co-inventors/
4. Bitcoin: A Peer-to-Peer Electronic Cash System https://blockchain-training.com/wp-content/uploads/2024/04/SatoshiNakamotoWhitePaper.pdf
5. In 1996, John Elkington coined the phrase *"The Triple Bottom Line"*. A business system needs to focus not only on Profit, but also on People and Planet. https://johnelkington.com/archive/TBL-elkington-chapter.pdf
6. Interoperability: *The ability of computer systems or software to exchange and make use of information. The ability of equipment or groups to operate in conjunction with each other.*

Chapter 1

Innovation

Innovation is change that unlocks new value.

– Jamie Notter[1]

Learning Objectives

Upon completing this chapter on Lean innovation, you will be able to:

- Explain Lean Kaizen, Lean Kaikaku, and Lean Kakushin
- Recognize the parallels between the rise of the internet and the emergence of Web 3.0
- Understand the concepts of "transformative change" and "radical change"
- Be clear on why Blockchain technology requires System Thinking and design thinking
- Follow the evolution of Organizational Structures over the past 100 years

Introduction

In this chapter, we explore Lean Kaizen, Lean Kaikaku, and Lean Kakushin to understand their pivotal roles in driving transformative change.

We will use as an example the transformative change that occurred in business and society as a result of the "World-Wide Web" internet during the 1990s and early 2000s.

DOI: 10.4324/9781003599715-1

A similar transformation is possible with the use of Web 3 and Blockchain technology in the 2020s and beyond.

Lean Kaizen, Kaikaku, and Kakushin strategies are presented as valuable tools for organizations that want to embrace the innovative potential of Web 3 and Blockchain technology.

The benefits of transitioning to Web 3, the integration of Lean thinking with blockchain, and the role of Lean innovation in the shift from ego-centered to eco-infrastructure organizations (ECO-ORGs) are key themes explored in this transformative journey.

Lean Transformation: Kaizen, Kaikaku, and Kakushin

Lean provides three distinct approaches to improvement, which have been named by the Japanese as Kaizen, Kaikaku, and Kakushin.

These three Japanese words represent the following:

- Kaizen: Small and regular changes for improvement; incremental improvement often in an iterative way.
- Kaikaku: Radical change that replaces a previous design/process/business model with a new design/process/business model.
- Kakushin: The use of innovation for transformational change, disruption of the status quo. It involves a paradigm shift, a new way of thinking and behaving.

Lean Kaizen

The term "Kaizen" is understood in Japanese as "Change for the good in small incremental steps", Kaizen (1986). In the context of Lean manufacturing, Lean Kaizen represents a culture and mindset within organizations for "Everybody, Everywhere, Every Day" Masaaki Imai "Kaizen, The Key to Japan's Competitive Success" (1986) to be identifying and making small improvements to the way in which work is being done.

Lean Kaikaku

The term "Kaikaku" translates to "radical change" or "revolution" in Japanese. In the context of Lean manufacturing, Lean Kaikaku represents a deliberate and strategic effort to bring about substantial and transformative changes within a process, system, or organization. Its goal is to swiftly enhance efficiency, quality, and overall performance. The methodology behind Lean Kaikaku involves a meticulous process of identifying bottlenecks, eliminating non-value-added activities, and re-engineering processes to achieve breakthrough results. This approach becomes valuable when incremental improvements (Kaizen) prove insufficient to overcome existing challenges, necessitating a more profound and sweeping transformation.

Lean Kakushin

"Kakushin" translates to "innovation" or "reform" in Japanese. Lean Kakushin centers around fostering a culture of innovation within an organization. It encourages employees at all levels to cultivate innovative ideas, experiment with diverse approaches, and actively contribute to the evolution of processes and products. Lean Kakushin places a strong emphasis on creating an environment that nurtures creativity, experimentation, and views failures as opportunities for learning. This approach is an organization's key to adapting to ever-changing market conditions and shifting customer needs while maintaining a competitive edge.

All three approaches—Lean Kaizen, Lean Kaikaku, and Lean Kakushin—hold integral positions within Lean thinking, concepts which have been used to their fullest effect by Toyota in its Toyota Production System. These principles have gained universal acceptance across various industries to enhance operational efficiency, reduce waste, improve quality, and ultimately create more value for all stakeholders.

Learning to See What Is Not There Yet

Blockchain technology and decentralized systems stand at the forefront of a transformative change, poised to revolutionize how we structure organizations and organize value transfers in processes. To grasp the profound implications of this shift, we think it helps to draw parallels with something we have experienced before: the advent of the internet. While these changes may have been challenging to foresee in advance, they appear highly logical when viewed in retrospect.

A Comparative Analysis

We can compare and contrast the rise of Web 3 and Blockchain technology to the rise of the Internet and Web 2 e-commerce.

Innovation and Evolution

With the internet, we created new ways of communication, entertainment, socialization, and business transactions. With Web 3.0 powered by Blockchain technology, we have created a decentralized record-keeping platform for value transfer and messaging. This innovation facilitates secure value transfers, digital asset management, and application development.

Decentralization or Disintermediation

Initially, the internet was dominated by centralized systems with a few major players. Blockchain and Web 3.0 aim to shift this paradigm by leveraging decentralized networks to reduce reliance on central authorities and empower individual users. This move from centralized control to decentralized control is often referred to as disintermediation because it removes *intermediaries* in transactions.

Value Transfer

While the internet transformed information communications, digital payments and value transfers continued to rely on traditional *legacy* financial systems. Web 3.0 leverages blockchain and cryptocurrencies to enable direct peer-to-peer value transfers, facilitating fast and cost-effective cross-border transactions.

Privacy and Identity

Concerns over online privacy and data security have become prominent. Web 3.0 addresses these concerns through decentralized identity systems and encrypted communication, offering users greater control over their personal information.

Innovation and Applications

Just as the internet sparked countless innovations, such as e-commerce and social networks, Web 3.0 opens the door to new functionality, including decentralized finance (DeFi), non-fungible tokens, decentralized apps (dApps), and *smart contracts (more about these new functionalities later in the book)*.

Adoption and Challenges

Just as the internet faced challenges in its early days, Web 3.0 grapples with issues like scalability, user-friendliness, and legal and regulatory hurdles. Web 3.0 is expected to evolve gradually, offering both new opportunities and challenges.

In summary, Web 3.0 has the potential to revolutionize how we transfer value, conduct transactions, and engage in digital interactions, much like how the internet reshaped information sharing and communication. As the internet gradually evolved, Web 3.0 is poised to follow a similar trajectory, bringing many new opportunities as well as challenges.

Transformative Innovation Is Here!

Lean Kaikaku and Lean Kakushin offer invaluable strategies for organizations seeking transformative improvements. Embracing these Lean principles can elevate efficiency, enhance quality, and foster innovation. As we continue this transformative journey, staying adaptable and innovative is key to thriving in this dynamic digital age.

Key Benefits of Transformation for Lean Practitioners

The transformation to blockchain-based transactional systems (Web 3.0) brings many benefits compared to traditional internet (Web 2.0)-based systems.

- ☐ Proof of ownership
- ☐ Proof of provenance
- ☐ Trust and transparency
- ☐ Enhanced privacy
- ☐ New incentive models
- ☐ New governance models

☐ Interoperability
☐ Censorship resistance
☐ Reduced middlemen and costs
☐ Global accessibility
☐ Immutable content
☐ Reduced data monopolies
☐ Control by design
☐ Security by design

DYOR is an acronym for "Do Your Own Research". DYOR is advice generally given to anyone getting involved in the cryptocurrency markets with real money, advising them to research topics on their own instead of simply believing some random Twitter (X) account, Facebook article, or YouTube influencer.

Lean Thinking: Value, Value Streams, Flow, Pull, Perfection, and Trust and Respect

Lean thinking encompasses the principles of value, value streams, flow, pull, perfection, and trust and respect. It places a strong emphasis on delivering value to customers, streamlining processes, maintaining a smooth workflow, producing based on demand, and striving for perfection by eliminating waste and improving quality. This comprehensive methodology has found widespread application across industries, resulting in increased productivity, cost reduction, enhanced quality, and a more engaged workforce that works with mutual trust and respect.

Lean System Thinking: Collaborative Technology

One reason we refer to *blockchain* as a *Lean system technology* is that the technology facilitates collaboration and removal of *silos*. Power and control are decentralized and not in the hands of a single or small group of entities.

Blockchain technology is at its best when multiple diverse parties must cooperate, trust cannot be assumed, and transactions or data require transparency, tamper-proofing, and validation by all participants.

Blockchain's greatest advantage over more traditional data systems lies in its ability to track transaction statuses across a network of diverse stakeholders, making this information accessible and verifiable by all participants. In this decentralized network, the time and occurrence of transactions become irrefutably documented. This capacity to verify transactions without intermediaries opens the door to groundbreaking opportunities for establishing trust on the internet. In a manner like the internet itself, blockchain is ushering in new organizational models, revenue structures, persuasive strategies, products, and customer interactions.

Blockchain technology, also called Distributed Ledger Technology, prevents control by a single entity or small group, ensuring decentralization and transparency.

We are still in the early stages of this transformative journey. At the time of writing this chapter, Blockchain technology is at a similar stage to the internet of the 1990s—not an easy solution for rapid change. Mainstream adoption will take some time (perhaps 5–10 more years) …. Just as the owner of a record store in 1985 could not envision music's digital accessibility, where it's paid for per stream, the adoption of blockchain hinges on gradual evolution rather than immediate revolution.

Paradigm Shift

Numerous processes withhold information from stakeholders based on distinct interests and objectives. Non-disclosure can be a deliberate strategic choice, integral to business models. Moreover, companies often compartmentalize into departments, functions, systems, or roles, further fragmenting information and internal power dynamics. This fragmentation through "silo thinking" and "silo organizing" obstructs the smooth flow of product, payment, and information streams, rendering processes less predictable. This unpredictability yields problems and challenges, which provide opportunities for Lean practitioners and consultants to introduce the concepts and technology of blockchain and Web 3.

The adverse effects of information fragmentation, characterized by fluctuating demand downstream, are referred to as the "Bullwhip" effect or whiplash effect within the supply chain. This phenomenon occurs when information arrives late, leading to automatic inventory fluctuations. Imagine the transformation if we shared critical information with our chain partners, such as customers providing real-time product feedback. This could dramatically impact lead times, quality, and customer satisfaction, as we will explore later. One can envision a "supermarket model" where all stakeholders gain insight into the "who, what, where, and when" of a process.

Blockchain technology provides a solution to the problem of information fragmentation and information silos, for example, upstream suppliers not having sufficient insights into the true fluctuation in downstream demand in a supply chain and therefore overcompensating, creating the "Bullwhip" effect.

Imagine the reduction in waste and gains in sustainability if we shared critical information in real-time with supply-chain stakeholders, partners, suppliers, and customers who need it to make decisions. When information is not shared, not complete, not correct, or is lost, this results in many wastes, as shown in Figure 1.1.

UNINTENDED WASTE (by design)

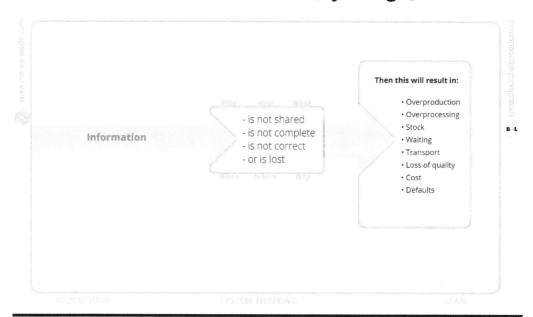

Figure 1.1 Wastes that result from poor quality of information inputs.

Machiel Tesser 2022

Lean Drivers Behind Blockchain

The elegance of this decentralized organizational model built on Blockchain technology lies in transparency, standardization, visualization, and accountability. Blockchain technology serves as the foundation, offering all process participants real-time insights into the flow of goods and work. This new insight into their processes and supply chains empowers every stakeholder involved to stay informed about the current status of their products or services.

For example, outsourced maintenance is jointly overseen by a company and an external service provider. Imagine if not only these two parties but also the customer could collaboratively monitor the entire process. This collaborative approach has the potential to yield positive results in terms of reduced lead times, enhanced quality, heightened customer satisfaction, and a lowered overall carbon footprint—all achievable by getting it right the first time and delivering just-in-time. It paves the way for greater efficiency and effectiveness of "Just-in-Time" using "Kanban", leading to improved flow with reduced waste.

This transformation is more about process design and organizational evolution than a mere technological challenge. Understanding this fundamental concept enables rapid assessment and adaptation, fostering progress and enhancements across various industries.

The Digital Transformation: Lean Innovation

Blockchain technology is transforming the "back office" of the internet. Blockchain digitizes registers of value, enabling value transactions to flow from one register to another in a seamless manner (the precise definition of "value" will be elaborated later).

Product flow, payment flow, and information flow can be synchronized to move at the same time and avoid the wastes of waiting and mistakes being made. See Figure 1.2.

Blockchain is the enabler for entirely new forms of value streams. This evolution aligns closely with the Lean philosophy of the frictionless flow of value streams.

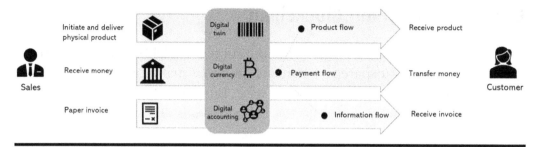

Figure 1.2   3-Flow model: Product flow, payment flow, and information flow.

Machiel Tesser 2020

Much like the internet, this transformation is progressing incrementally. The trend is unmistakable. This book explains these changes and their consequences for business and society. This book highlights the intersection of Lean thinking and Blockchain technology. We draw parallels with the rise of the internet, and we see that Blockchain technology is the foundation for a comparable radical transformation.

The Trend Is Your Friend: From dot.com to block.com Bubbles

The Dot-com crash of 2001 mirrors the crypto crash of 2018 and 2022. In 2001, the internet's potential was initially overestimated, resulting in an initial price bubble. In hindsight, this bubble was the opportune moment to invest in stocks like Amazon, Google, or Facebook. Like the rise of the internet, Blockchain technology has experienced fluctuations in perceived potential and subsequent price movements.

The rise of the internet started with the Internet Protocol TCP/IP in the 1960s, then the first use case (email) in the 1980s, followed by e-commerce in the 1990s. For the e-commerce on the internet to reach maturity, it took 45 years. We are only 17 years since the first blockchain was launched, so we can expect many more years before it becomes mainstream for use in our business applications. See Figure 1.3.

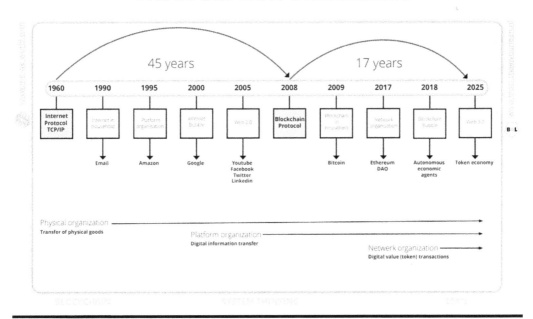

Figure 1.3   Timeline of Protocols and Applications from 1960 to 2025.

Machiel Tesser

Learn About Lean System Design Thinking

Just as you can explain the function of a car as a means of transportation, soon you'll be able to explain blockchain's function in terms of a superhighway for value flows, an enabler for collaboration, a foundation for trust and collaboration. An IT platform with built-in security by design that is superior to any existing network security models. While Lean principles are currently applied to centrally coordinated organizational structures, we aim to inspire decentralized organization through this book—for a leaner and more sustainable future.

We are entering an era where the ceaseless pursuit of more ("The acquisitive society") is losing its appeal to many. We are entering an era where "Fake News" is being exposed, and people are demanding evidence and have a thirst for the truth. We will not trust the free-range eggs based on packaging or Nike sneakers based on the "Swoosh" mark. We are transitioning from ego-centered organizations to eco-centered organizations, where contribution and collaboration lead to value, motivation, recognition, and reward, creating a leaner, fairer, and more inclusive society. This is what Lean Kakushin and blockchain innovation can do for us.

We'll Also Assist in Preventing You from Getting FOMO!

FOMO is an acronym for "Fear of Missing Out": the fear of not being included in something (such as an interesting or enjoyable activity) that others are experiencing.

In order for blockchain with Lean and Systems Thinking to be adopted, we must be able to answer the question, "What's in it for me?" A useful exercise is to see how many of the checkboxes shown in Figure 1.4 you answer "yes" to for your business processes.

■ **Control by design**

Personal information is protected against identity theft and fraud. Give only the part of your identity that is needed. For example, to enter a bar or nightclub, you can prove your age without also needing to provide your name and address.[9]

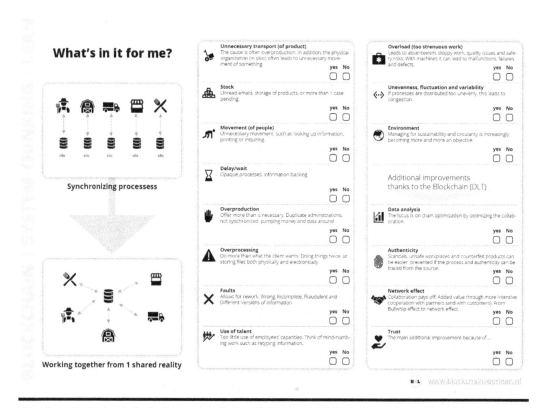

Figure 1.4 What's in it for me? Advantages of working from a shared reality.

Machiel Tesser (2020)

■ **Privacy**

Take control of your digital footprint and decide who has access to your personal information. With digital identity, privacy is not just a promise; it is a fundamental right.

■ **Empowerment without waste (of time)**

With the ability to assert your identity across domains, wasted time is removed from the process. Lead times for processing documents and applications can be reduced by orders of magnitude.

Summary

Lean goes beyond only continuous improvement, Lean Kaizen. Lean also encourages radical change and innovation through Lean Kaikaku and Lean Kakushin.

Comparing the Internet and Web 2.0 revolution with the Blockchain and Web 3.0 revolution helps with our understanding. Also, by applying the concept of decentralized organizations, we obtain an insight into the future of Lean organizational structures.

Significant Lean benefits from moving to Web 3.0 include proof of ownership, improved privacy, new incentive and governance models, fewer handovers (middlemen: constraints in value flow), and global accessibility to information for those who need it and have permissions.

We also recognize that the complexity of this concept does not allow for a simple and concise "elevator pitch". The same applied to explaining the internet when it first appeared. To fully understand these concepts, extensive reading, questioning, and individual research (DYOR) are needed.

Within our traditional organizational framework (TRAD-ORG), inefficiencies and waste persist as a result of information fragmentation, siloed behaviors, and push models. By embracing blockchain as a Lean system concept, the focus shifts from a competitive organizational model towards a collaborative model. Transparency and cooperation will become the new norm.

The future state, as suggested in this chapter, involves the transition from a self-centered competitive organization to an eco-infrastructure organization. In this new model, rewards and incentives are given for behaviors that benefit the entire system. This helps to promote a more inclusive and fairer society, which is in alignment with SDG and other sustainability goals.

WAGMI is an acronym for the phrase "We're All Gonna Make It". It is a slang term used on social media platforms among traders and investors to convey a sense of optimism or encouragement.

Note

1. Jamie Notter: https://www.forbes.com/sites/forbescoachescouncil/2021/01/12/how-to-build-a-culture-of-innovation

Chapter 2

Purpose

Optimizing ecosystem value through Lean, Blockchain, and Systems Thinking

Introduction

David J. Morris[1] observed that in the perpetual race between technology and ethics, the advantage consistently goes to technology.

As we witness remarkable technological advancements, our ethical capacities struggle to keep pace.

This chapter explains the purpose of Lean thinking with Blockchain technology and Systems Thinking for providing an ethical way to achieve sustainable productivity, growth, and development.

DOI: 10.4324/9781003599715-2

Learning Objectives

Upon completing this chapter, you will be familiar with:

- The purpose of Lean
- Identifying value and waste in processes
- Methods to eliminate waste strategically
- Improving flow
- The purpose of blockchains
- Identifying ecosystem value through decentralization
- Eliminating systems' waste with blockchain
- Improving collaborative flow with blockchain

The Purpose of Lean

Lean creates value while conserving resources and minimizing waste. In contrast to the common practice of always attempting to maximize resource utilization, Lean focuses on finding optimal resource utilization, that is not 100%, for the benefit of the entire system.

Lean is not just a set of tools; it is a comprehensive, philosophical, and systemic approach.

Identifying Value and Waste in Processes

One common definition of "value" is any action or process that a stakeholder is willing to pay for. This chapter emphasizes the importance of delivering high-quality products or services by maximizing value while minimizing waste.

Japanese production guru Taiichi Ohno[2] suggested that waste (or "muda" in Japanese) has seven main categories. An eighth category of waste is also commonly considered to be an important consideration: the waste of skills, talent, and ideas of workers.

Let's define these categories of waste and see what *process improvements* could reduce these wastes.

1. Overproduction

Producing more than requested or producing earlier than planned can lead to excess inventory, higher storage costs, and waste because products become outdated or expired over time. Keep in mind that overproduction often comes from insufficient or a lack of real-time information or because of "just-in-case" management.

Improvements

By improving the **transparency and accuracy of information**, companies can reduce the risks associated with overproduction. The Lean principle of producing the right amount of products at the right time and with the right resources is called "just-in-time" management. This requires **just-in-time information**.

2. Waiting

Delays in processes, whether due to idle time or waiting for materials, information, or approvals, can significantly impact operational efficiency and productivity. When workers are left waiting for the next step in a process, valuable time is wasted, leading to increased lead times, reduced throughput, and higher costs. Waiting is a symptom of a lack of flow in the process design.

Improvements

Investing in advanced technologies that improve communication, collaboration, and coordination, such as disintermediation, represents a clear path to significantly accelerate the reduction of wait times. Think of removing the intermediary by introducing a real-time information board, functioning as an automative trusted traffic light. This will replace all the actions that go along with intermediation, removing the opening hours, waiting times, the verification and authorization processes, etc.

Example: *Email as Waste*

Email, despite being a prevalent communication tool, can introduce inefficiencies in Lean processes. Traditional email systems often lead to delays, miscommunication, and information silos, hindering the smooth flow of information within organizations.

Lack of Real-Time Collaboration

Email limits real-time collaboration, which is essential for agile decision-making and problem-solving. Without instant communication channels, teams may struggle to address issues promptly, leading to delays in process improvement and decision implementation.

Lack of Real-Time Communication

Email poses significant challenges in ensuring data integrity and security. Emails can be vulnerable to hacks, phishing attacks, and data breaches, compromising sensitive information critical for Lean operations. Maintaining the integrity of data throughout the supply chain is important for achieving Lean objectives. This is difficult to ensure through traditional email systems.

Lack of Real-Time Coordination

In Lean processes, transparency and traceability are essential for identifying bottlenecks, monitoring progress, and ensuring accountability across the supply chain. Without these capabilities, organizations may struggle to optimize processes effectively.

Email's limitations become more pronounced when considering blockchain solutions. Blockchain technology offers decentralized, secure, and transparent communication channels that align closely with Lean principles. Unlike email, blockchain facilitates real-time collaboration, ensures data integrity through cryptographic techniques, and provides transparent, immutable records of transactions. By leveraging blockchain solutions, organizations can overcome the shortcomings of email and achieve greater efficiency, security, and transparency in Lean processes.

3. Transport

Transportation (**as a waste**) is the unnecessary movement of materials or products between locations. It can significantly impact operational efficiency, increase costs, and contribute to environmental concerns such as carbon emissions. When materials or products are transported unnecessarily, it adds both time and expense to the production process, leading to delays, inefficiencies, and loss of resources.

Improvements

To address transportation inefficiencies and minimize its negative impacts, companies must adopt strategies to optimize logistics and reduce the unnecessary movement of materials and products. Improving supply chain visibility and transparency can greatly help optimize transportation. Also access to accurate quality information is of crucial importance.

Example

The blockage of the Suez Canal in 2021 by the container ship Ever Given highlights inefficiencies in transportation. It shows that access to accurate information plays a pivotal role in improving transportation **efficiency, resilience, and risk management**. By leveraging timely insights and proactive strategies, stakeholders can optimize operational performance, mitigate disruptions and risks, and ensure the seamless flow of goods and commodities across global supply chains.

4. Overprocessing

Overprocessing is about doing more work than necessary or using more resources than required to complete a task. It also applies to over-complicating or over-engineering a process. When processes are over-processed, valuable resources such as time, labor, materials, and energy are wasted on activities that do not contribute to the final outcome. This results in wasted efforts, longer cycle times, and higher operational expenses. Furthermore, overprocessing can lead to diminished quality and customer satisfaction.

Improvements

Transparency, industry standards, and access to accurate information are critical to preventing overprocessing. There are limitations in our current system design that make it challenging, such as:

Communication: The system is competitively driven, preventing information sharing.

Coordination: Multiple stakeholders have their own vertical, siloed perspective, systems, and goals.

Cooperation: Cultures, rules, and legislation are not aligned.

5. Unnecessary Inventory

Maintaining too much inventory beyond what is needed ties up valuable resources and takes up space that could be used more effectively. Additionally, as inventory ages, it loses its quality, leading to potential losses and even more waste. Inventories are often the result of **push system designs**.

In a push system, products are made based on forecasts or guesses about what customers might want. This often leads to overproduction and wasted resources because items are made before there is a demand for them.

In a pull system, products are made only when there is a specific demand for them. This means production is driven by actual customer orders or needs. It helps to minimize waste and ensures that products are made when they are needed, reducing work-in-progress (WIP), excess inventory, and unecessary costs. Push is more about guessing **what customers want**, while pull is about making and delivering **what customers actually need**.

Improvements

With a pull system design, you can better understand inventory levels, demand patterns, and supply chain dynamics. This ensures that companies can make informed decisions about inventory levels and allocation. Due to its peer-to-peer system design, Blockchain technology is exceptionally well-suited for implementing **a pull system for information retrieval**.

6. Unnecessary Motion

Wasteful movements of people or equipment within processes, known as motion waste, can lead to inefficiencies, increased operational costs, and reduced productivity. Unnecessary motion not only consumes valuable time and energy but also increases the risk of errors, accidents, and injuries.

7. Defects

Defects, errors, and mistakes within processes can result in rework, scrap, delays, and additional costs, all of which hinder operational efficiency and profitability. When products do not meet quality standards, they either have to undergo costly rework to resolve the problems or are discarded as scrap.

Improvements

With Blockchain technology, the focus on total quality is becoming increasingly important. This total quality also includes social, ecological, and sustainable aspects. The goal is to authenticate and validate quality at the source, while embedding ownership, accountability, and traceability into the system design.

8. Waste of Skills, Talent, and Ideas

When the skills, talents, and ideas of employees are not fully utilized or deployed effectively, it's also a form of waste. This underutilization can lead to missed opportunities for innovation, decreased employee engagement and potential, reduced productivity, and the creation of unnecessary bureaucratic roles.

How often is the creative thinking of employees ignored due to insufficient listening, undermining support for change, and limiting decision-making solely to managers? Achieving success requires the commitment and support of the management toward all workers where value is created, "The Gemba".[3]

Improvements

Generating a culture of trust and mutual respect extends beyond mere manifesto rhetoric to tangible action from all involved.

Gemba (現場) is the Japanese term for "actual place", often used for the shop floor or any place where value-creating work actually occurs.[4]

Additional Categories of Waste

The emergence of Blockchain technology reveals additional forms of waste beyond the traditional eight Lean wastes. These include inadequate decision-making and knowledge sharing, waste of time due to our organizational model (Web 2.0), waste created by ineffective systems design, people being used as products, wasted information, and inefficient resource management. There will be more than mentioned here, but these are the most important.

Methods to Eliminate Waste Strategically

To strategically eliminate or reduce identified wastes in Lean methodologies, a systematic and proactive approach is taken, utilizing key principles and methods. These strategies are designed to continuously improve processes and contribute to overall efficiency. Below are some crucial techniques used in Lean to effectively address and eliminate waste.

Value Stream Mapping

Value Stream Mapping serves as a visual representation of the entire process, from customer order to delivery. By visualizing each step and mapping out the flow of materials and information, this tool becomes crucial in identifying waste and inefficiencies.

Organizations can strategically focus on improvements by simplifying, visualizing, and optimizing processes, reducing unnecessary steps and complexities.

Visualization and Feedback Loops

The practice of producing or delivering items in smaller batch sizes, or even one at a time when necessary, ensures that the wastes of unnecessary inventory and overproduction are reduced. The integration of feedback loops is crucial in this regard. See Figure 2.1.

In Lean practices, Kanban is a widely employed visual management method, utilizing cards or signals to control the seamless flow of materials and information. Digital adaptations of this approach, such as notifications,

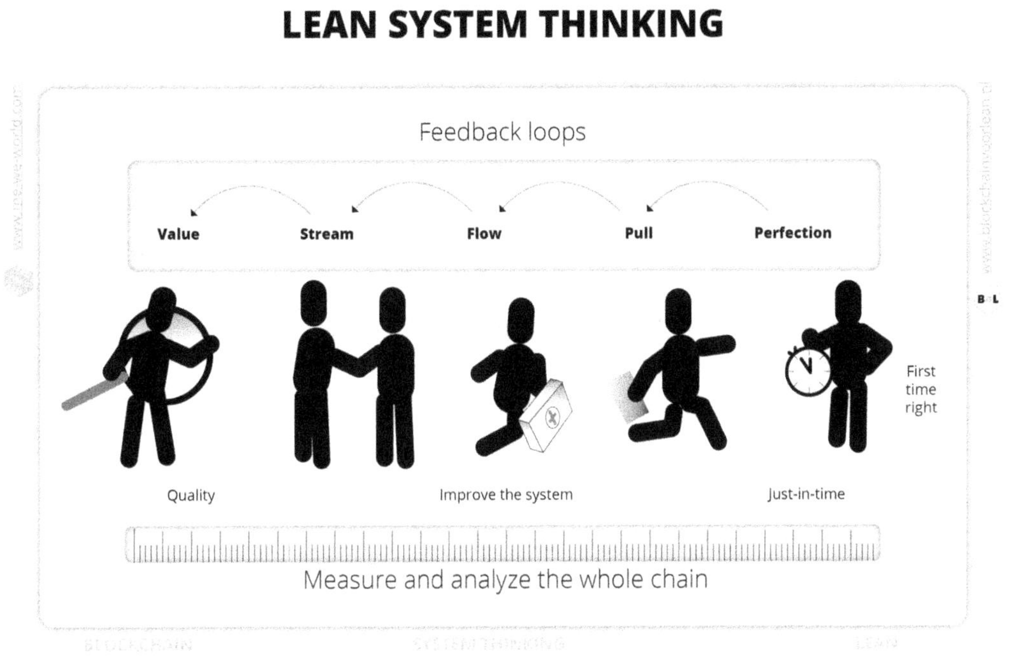

LEAN SYSTEM THINKING

Figure 2.1 The integration of feedback loops within the Lean framework.

Machiel Tesser (2020)

sounds, or pop-ups, have demonstrated remarkable efficiency, offering the advantage of receiving and accessing updates regardless of one's **location**. Notably, these digital signals are frequently leveraged as **incentives**, acting as a motivational mechanism to accomplish tasks.

Standardization

Standardization ensures that tasks and activities are performed consistently and uniformly. When everyone follows the same standardized procedures and quality standards, there is less room for variation or errors in the process. This consistency not only contributes to the reliability of outcomes but also enhances customer satisfaction, meeting their expectations for a certain level of quality and reliability. Additionally, standardization helps organizations in complying with legal requirements and industry standards, reducing the risk of non-compliance issues.

Standardization provides a structured and systematic approach toward achieving the purpose of a process. It establishes a foundation for improvement, efficiency, and consistency. This, in turn, contributes to the overall success of an organization by making process results more predictable.

Continuous Improvement (Kaizen)

Cultivating a culture of continuous improvement is pivotal in Lean methodologies. Employees are encouraged to identify and implement small changes that improve efficiency and reduce waste. This approach involves making incremental adjustments to processes on an ongoing basis. Employees at all levels play an active role in suggesting improvements and participating in problem-solving activities, thereby contributing to the elimination of waste. This commitment to continuous improvement aligns with Lean principles and ensures that processes remain dynamic and responsive to evolving challenges and opportunities.

Poka-Yoke (Error Proofing)

Poka-Yoke involves designing processes or systems to prevent errors or defects from occurring. By implementing mechanisms that detect and prevent mistakes before they escalate, Poka-Yoke ensures smoother flow and higher-quality output.

The above techniques collectively contribute to waste reduction, process improvement, and overall organizational success in Lean methodologies. In the next section, we will explain how our traditional organizational design prevents seamless flow in processes.

Improving the Flow of Value

In Lean methodology, "flow" refers to the smooth and uninterrupted movement of value in processes from start to finish, without delays, interruptions, or wasteful activities. It is about optimizing the sequence of activities to minimize bottlenecks and constraints and deliver value to customers as quickly as possible. This section explores the constraints induced by handover processes and intermediary involvement.

Understanding the impact of handovers or intermediary involvement on value flow is crucial for Lean and Systems Thinking. Let's delve deeper into these constraints.

Handovers (Transfer Points) Interrupt the Flow

A handover or transfer point is where work is transferred from one area of responsibility to another. Every handover inherently leads to delays and the chance of loss of information, creating waiting times and extra (control) work. These waiting times increase the overall process lead time, reduce efficiency, and create a bottleneck for improving flow.

The question we may ask ourselves is, why do we use a push system for information transfer? Why are we still using paper receipts and emailing as communication and coordination mechanisms?

 "The most dangerous kind of waste is the waste we don't recognize". Shigeo Shingo[5]

■ Miscommunication due to information loss

Each handover introduces the potential for miscommunication or **information loss**. As work moves from one team or individual to another, there is a risk of details being misunderstood, overlooked, or not adequately communicated. In a world where data is valued as money or knowledge, there is a danger that certain data may not be shared. This leads to data errors, rework, control activities, or a need for clarification.

Do you think the intensive use of email could be the result of an information backlog?

■ Adaptability and agility challenges

Working with handovers often results in a push system. In a push system, work is pushed to the next stage regardless of its demand. This lack of responsiveness to actual demand will again result in all kinds of waste, such as overproduction, overprocessing, and defects, as mentioned in the first paragraph of this chapter.

■ Transitioning to a pull system

Addressing these issues involves transitioning from **a push system to a pull system design** without handovers. In a pull system, work is initiated based on actual demand, based on real time information from customers to suppliers. This shift enhances adaptability and agility, mitigates waiting times, and minimizes the risk of miscommunication.

The Lean methodology serves as a comprehensive framework aimed at optimizing resource use, streamlining process flow, and systematically eliminating waste. By embracing Lean principles and methodologies alongside a continuous improvement mindset, organizations ensure consistent alignment of processes with customer needs and organizational goals.

Management support is crucial for successful Lean implementation because decisions must be in harmony with the organization's purpose, objectives, and vision.

Embracing Lean Thinking

Effective implementation of Lean principles throughout a supply chain is usually prevented by poor collaboration and communication and a lack of a common goal among stakeholders. Embracing "Lean thinking" is critical. To embrace this approach effectively, all relevant stakeholders must be brought together to look for "win-win-win" scenarios and to answer questions such as:

■ What are the causes of waiting times, overprocessing, and overproduction?
■ Why don't we have standardized procedures?
■ What is the biggest constraint in the flow of value?

Most of those problems won't be solved if there is no motivation or incentive to collaborate. The past 40 years have instead encouraged a "winner take all" and a "win-lose-lose" mentality.

Round Tables

Examining the supply chain with a round table discussion or "Quality Circle"[6] could help to align the diverse needs and objectives of stakeholders. Needs and objectives are referred to as "Voices" by Lean practitioners. These voices include customers, suppliers, environmental concerns, special interest groups, shareholders, management, and workers.

Ignoring these diverse voices and ignoring the end-to-end process design leads to waste by design. Therefore, addressing the concerns of all stakeholders through Lean System Thinking (LST) is essential for improving efficiency and effectiveness within the supply chain.

Furthermore, it is critical to recognize the work and activities that should not exist in the first place, known in Lean as "non-value-adding activities". Consider improving the intermediary's processes, while a new innovation makes the intermediary redundant.

Learning to understand a decentralized way of organizing is crucial to understand tasks that actually contribute to value creation.

To summarize, if we want to design a Lean system infrastructure, it is important to listen to all the voices within the whole network.

Before designing a process, it is critical to establish the values at stake and identify the relevant stakeholders. In the field of Blockchain technology, the effectiveness of an application depends on a deep understanding of the system's functionality, requirements, and sustainable goals.

When deploying blockchain, emphasis is placed on rules and protocols. These serve as guiding principles for cohesive collaboration towards common objectives, ensuring that inputs are reliably translated into desired outcomes through repeatable processes.

Effective alignment on shared goals requires clarity on how to act, solve problems, and make decisions consistently and reliably.

In the context of Lean methodologies, these operational guidelines are called standard operating procedures; within the domain of Blockchain, they are called protocols or algorithms. It is critical to recognize that blockchain serves as a tool within a system, rather than a standalone solution, that enables collaborative efforts for shared purposes.

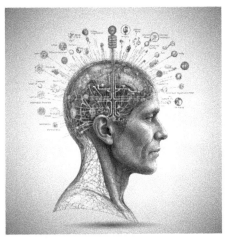

"Algorithms are arguably the single most important concept in our world. If we want to understand our life and our future, we should make every effort to understand what an algorithm is and how algorithms are connected with emotions. An algorithm is a methodical set of steps that can be used to make calculations, resolve problems, and reach decisions. An algorithm isn't a particular calculation, but the method followed when making the calculation".
Yuval Noah Harari[7]

In this chapter, we are exploring the role of blockchain as a community tool, closely aligned with the community's goals. We emphasize the importance of doing things right the first time, just-in-time, and functioning with a collaborative mentality.

Blockchains facilitate decentralization and maximize ecosystem value. Decentralized design removes the biggest constraint in value flows: intermediaries. Blockchain technology enables seamless **one-piece flow** and can be aligned with **diverse perspectives and values as long as there is a common goal (mission).**

Today's value streams are often complex and interconnected to varying degrees.

The effectiveness of these value streams depends largely on the degree of cooperation that is in line with a shared mission and vision, the skill of communication, and the skill with which interactions are orchestrated. These critical factors can be summarized as the "three Cs" of collaboration, coordination, and communication. Web 3.0 digitalization facilitates each of these components. See Figure 2.2.

A blockchain concept is based on collaborative design. This is a fundamentally different starting point than all traditional internet-based (TRAD-ORG) process designs. There is no real collaboration in competitively designed processes. This also causes all the waste we mentioned earlier in this chapter.

To prevent this waste, we will conduct a stakeholder analysis and a value stream analysis for the entire ecosystem. In addition, we will use Blockchain technology as a neutral system of which no one centralised entity is in charge. The transformation takes place **from trust in centralized**

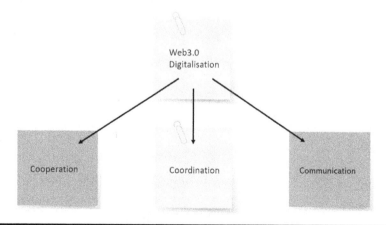

Figure 2.2　The "three Cs" of Web 3 digitalization.

intermediaries to trust in decentralized concensus mechanisms and cryptography. A real Lean Kakushin event!

To understand a blockchain ecosystem, we will explain **five components** that make up the "system".

Identifying Ecosystem Value Through the "5R"

Let's explore the five R's of the system: Roles, Relationships, Resources, Rules, and Results.

Roles

Blockchain revolutionizes identity and interaction tracking (the relationship), establishing a transparent ecosystem where every entity—be it individuals, corporations, products, or even objects like a refrigerator or a tree—holds a unique identity, voice, and stake.

Mapping all the roles in the system is the first step in developing the deeper understanding of relationships and dependencies between them. Understanding roles of all stakeholders protects against the power of individual interests at the expense of the whole system and provides effective control measures for the long term.

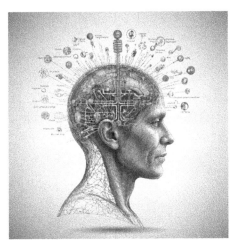

"Systems thinking is a discipline for seeing wholes. It is a framework for seeing interrelationships rather than things, for seeing 'patterns of change' rather than static 'snapshots'".
– Peter Senge[8]

Relationships

The interdependencies between identities are based on their relationships and interactions. It is vital to see that we depend on each other, not only financially, but also socially and for the preservation of the planet. This becomes clearer through a blockchain stakeholder analysis.

Let's explore this concept with a simple supply chain example:

Suppose you are designing a blockchain solution for a supply chain network, where various entities such as manufacturers, suppliers, distributors, and retailers are involved. Each participant in the network is assigned a unique cryptographic key that serves as their digital identity.

Supplier

The blockchain records transactions related to the supply of materials from the supplier to the manufacturer, linking them to their respective identities.

Manufacturer

When the manufacturer produces a batch of products, it records this information on the blockchain, associating the transaction with its unique identity.

Distributor

Transactions involving the movement of goods from the manufacturer through the distributor to the retailer are recorded on the blockchain, with each participant's identity being crucial for verification.

Retailer

Transactions related to product sales and inventory management are recorded on the blockchain, tying each activity back to the retailer's identity. The interdependencies between identities become evident in the following ways:

Chain of Custody

The blockchain creates a transparent and immutable ledger that shows the entire chain of custody for a product. It manages the **in and out flows of stock** during the whole process. Each identity is linked to the corresponding transactions, ensuring **a traceable history**.

Verification and Trust

Participants can verify the authenticity of transactions by checking the cryptographic signatures associated with each identity. This builds trust among network participants.

Consensus of Predefined Rules and Conditions

Smart contracts, self-executing contracts with the terms of the agreement directly written into code, often involve multiple parties. These contracts rely on the identities of the participants to enforce predefined rules and conditions.

The interdependencies between identities in a blockchain solution for a supply chain illustrate how each participant's unique digital identity is crucial for establishing trust, ensuring transparency, and maintaining the integrity of the distributed ledger. If the intention is to make the network more social or sustainable, then it is a matter of adjusting the rules to focus on these additional values. **Competition should take place at the network level rather than at the corporate level**.

Resources

Blockchain technology is an enabler in advancing beyond traditional analysis, offering a holistic view of the entire ecosystem, revealing not only relationships but also the movement and accumulation of value, behaviors, rules, regulations, and objectives. This holistic approach, known as Lean System Thinking, explores the interconnectedness of all stakeholders and their contributions. This is crucial for assessing sustainable systems where our carbon footprint is an increasingly important part of how we define value and success.

Blockchain technology manages the whole instead of the parts. Blockchain is the "How" and the "Where" which stores the truth about the "Who", "What", "When", and "Why". See Figure 2.3.

Rules

The rules of a blockchain concept are essentially the set of protocols, algorithms, and consensus mechanisms that govern the behavior of the network.

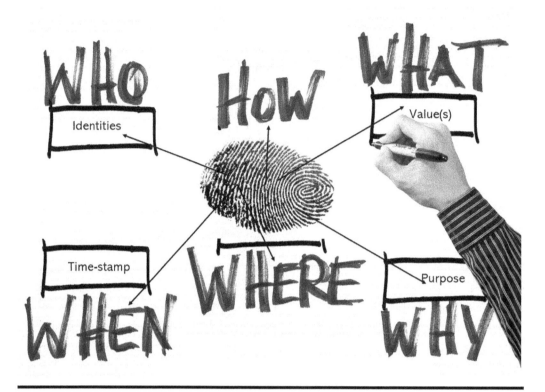

Figure 2.3 Blockchain is the "How" and the "Where" which stores the truth about the "Who", "What", "When", and "Why".

These rules are designed to ensure the security, integrity, and consensus of the distributed ledger.

"To manage a system effectively, you might focus on the interactions of the parts rather than their behaviour taken separately".
– Russell L. Ackoff[9]

Here are the key aspects related to the rules of a blockchain:

Consensus Mechanism

A consensus mechanism is a protocol that enables nodes in a decentralized network to agree on the state of the blockchain. It ensures that all participants have a consistent view of the ledger.

Cryptography

Cryptographic techniques, such as hashing and digital signatures, are employed to secure transactions and control access to the blockchain. These techniques ensure the immutability of the ledger and protect against tampering.

 Hash functions are used to create unique identifiers for blocks, and digital signatures verify the authenticity of transactions.

Smart Contracts

Smart contracts are self-executing contracts with the terms of the agreement directly written into code. They enforce predefined rules and automate processes within the blockchain.

Consistency and Immutability

The blockchain maintains a consistent and immutable history of transactions. Once a block is added to the chain, it cannot be altered, ensuring the integrity of the entire ledger.

Decentralization

Blockchain networks are designed to be decentralized, meaning no single entity has control over the entire network. Decentralization enhances security and resilience against attacks.

Governance Models

Governance models determine how decisions are made regarding protocol upgrades, rule changes, and network modifications. Some blockchains have decentralized governance structures, while others may have more centralized control.

Tokenomics

Many blockchains use native tokens as a means of value transfer, access to network features, or participation in governance. Token economics define how tokens are created, distributed, and used within the ecosystem.

These rules collectively shape the behavior of a blockchain, facilitating secure transactions, decentralized governance, and the execution of programmable agreements through smart contracts. The rules ensure that the system operates in a trustless and transparent manner while maintaining the integrity of the distributed ledger. All these elements contribute to making the result more predictable; manage the purpose!

Results

Blockchain technology **transforms value stream identification** within ecosystems by establishing transparent records of identities and interactions. It enables every entity, human or non-human, to have a distinct identity and involvement. This transparency facilitates a deeper understanding of relationships, needs, and objectives among entities, empowering a more inclusive and comprehensive ecosystem analysis, aligning perfectly with Lean methodologies' goals.

Another benefit is that immutable data storage facilitates the creation of value stream histories. **This is the missing part for creating a circular economy** in which we can track, trace, and analyze the value of the whole lifecycle.

Web3 represents a paradigm shift in how value is identified and exchanged. A groundbreaking aspect of Web3 is enabling machines, physical or digital, to autonomously participate in economic activities. Through smart contracts and token incentives, machines can perform tasks and receive rewards, allowing them to cover operational costs, becoming self-sufficient entities.

In this context, an autonomous car functioning as a taxi can receive direct payments for its services, managing its expenses using earned tokens for electric charging and maintenance. Web3 fosters new business models where machines become active economic agents, reshaping traditional value flows and paving the way for a decentralized and incentivized future economy.

From Digitizing to Digitalization

Understanding the difference between digitizing (Web 2.0) and digitalization (Web 3.0) is important when discussing the use of Blockchain technology.

Digitizing describes the process of converting analog data into digital format, exemplified by activities such as scanning physical documents or images.

Digitalization describes the utilization of digital technologies to overhaul existing operational procedures. Digitalization clarifies relationships between identities, promoting the creation of skin in the game process designs centered around shared priorities with established consensus.

Both digitization and digitalization play an integral role in facilitating a company's journey towards digital transformation.

Eliminating Systems' Waste with Blockchain

Blockchain is emerging as a transformative force in the next wave of improvement for business, government, and society, eradicating inefficiencies and waste by harnessing the power of **collaboration, coordination, and communication**.

Blockchain distributed ledger technology revolutionizes the way stakeholders interact, aligning their goals and motivations with shared purposes while streamlining processes. Eliminating waste within these value streams is fundamental to the core principles of Lean blockchain.

Trust the Process

Blockchain creates trust with its decentralized design together with its robust consensus mechanisms and cryptography. It removes the necessity for trusted intermediaries or centralized authorities.

Conventional systems rely on intermediaries such as banks, brokers, or administrators for transaction verification and record-keeping, leading to slow, costly, and error-prone processes. Settlements, the finalization of transactions, can take weeks due to the complexity of synchronizing information across diverse systems and taxonomies.

Multiple Value(s) Integrations

Blockchain is a collaborative technology and can focus **on multiple values** beyond just financial values. Examples of ecosystem values are contained in the 17 Sustainable Development Goals (SDGs) established by the United Nations (UN) to create a better world by 2030.

These 17 goals focus on key areas such as poverty, health, education, equality, climate change, and peace. These goals aim to promote social progress, environmental protection, and prosperity for everyone. Their success requires global action, investments, and policies at local, national, and international levels.

Let's consider some initiatives leveraging blockchain for specific SDG initiatives:

Climate action (SDG 13)
Blockchain technology offers several innovative solutions for climate action. Here are some blockchain solutions that contribute to addressing climate-related challenges:

- Carbon credits and emissions tracking: Ensuring the accurate tracking of emissions reduction efforts, making it easier for organizations to buy and sell verified carbon credits.
- Supply chain transparency: Tracing the origin and journey of products in the supply chain. This allows consumers to verify the authenticity of eco-friendly claims and encourages companies to adopt sustainable practices throughout their supply chains.
- Renewable energy trading: Creating decentralized energy marketplaces using blockchain to facilitate peer-to-peer trading of renewable energy. This empowers individuals and businesses to buy and sell excess renewable energy directly, fostering a more sustainable and decentralized energy ecosystem.
- Climate impact investment with impact tokens: Utilizing blockchain to establish transparent and auditable records of climate impact investments, these key advantages effectively tackle challenges in impact investing, thereby contributing to narrowing the financing gap for SDGs.
- Tree planting and carbon offsetting: Record and validate tree-planting activities and carbon offset projects. Preventing green washing activities.

■ *Poverty alleviation (SDG 1)*
Implementations in Latin American countries provide digital identities for accessing basic services, reducing costs for the underprivileged.

■ *Decent work and economic growth (SDG 8) & responsible production and consumption (SDG 12)*
Blockchain ensures ethical production by tracing the supply chain, promoting fair trade, and increasing financing for disadvantaged sectors.

■ *Zero hunger (SDG 2)*
Programs like Sweden's track fund usage to ensure resources are allocated for specific purposes, such as combating child malnutrition.

■ *Peace, justice, and strong institutions (SDG 16)*
Blockchain's ability to enable programmable money offers governments and institutions a range of tools to improve financial processes, enhance transparency, and address specific challenges in the management and execution of monetary policies and financial transactions. Blockchain's transparency helps monitor public budgeting, reducing corruption and malpractices.

■ *Health and well-being (SDG 3)*
Blockchain in healthcare ensures secure and tamper-resistant data storage, enhancing privacy for sensitive information like patient records. It promotes interoperability by providing a standardized and secure method for sharing healthcare data, facilitating better coordination of patient care.

Identity management using blockchain ensures accurate and secure identification of patients and healthcare providers, preventing identity theft and streamlining administrative processes. In supply chain management, blockchain enhances transparency and traceability, tracking the production, distribution, and authentication of pharmaceuticals. For clinical trials and research, blockchain streamlines data management, ensuring the integrity and transparency of results while enabling efficient and secure data sharing among institutions.

■ *Affordable and clean energy (SDG 7)*
Blockchain enables the traceability of energy sources, tracks CO_2 footprints, and facilitates energy management and bonus programs.

These *applications* showcase how Blockchain technology could be an enabler for various SDGs by implementing transparency, accountability, and efficiency across different sectors, ultimately contributing to global sustainable development.

Improving Collaborative Flow with Blockchain

There are several elements of blockchain that work together to create a collaborative flow of value: token incentives, token marketing, tokenization, standards, smart contracts, pull systems, and feedback loops.

Voice of the Network (Stakeholder Analysis)

Lean methodology emphasizes the voices of the business and the customer (VOB and VOC), whereas blockchain transcends this approach by encompassing the entire ecosystem, the **voice of the ecosystem**, and **voice of the network**.

Blockchain brings **a broader and more inclusive perspective** than by using Lean alone.

Token Incentives

Tokens on a blockchain serve various purposes, one of which is incentivizing desired behavior within the network. Participants can earn tokens by contributing resources, performing specific tasks, or validating transactions (in the case of proof of stake or proof of work mechanisms). These incentives encourage network participants to act in ways that benefit the ecosystem, promoting network growth and integrity.

Token Marketing

Tokens symbolize ownership, transforming individuals **into stakeholders** within networks, which has become the new organizational paradigm. When users hold partial ownership, their motivation to contribute and propagate the message intensifies. This explains the pervasive "marketing" across platforms like LinkedIn, Discord, TikTok, and Twitter (X). Tokens are inseparable from marketing strategy; they serve as both the marketing tool and the reward mechanism that fuels marketing efforts.

Tokenization

Tokenization involves representing real-world assets, rights, or values digitally on a blockchain. These digital tokens can **represent various assets** such as currencies, securities, real estate, or even ownership **rights**. Tokenization facilitates the efficient transfer, exchange, and tracking of these assets on a blockchain and also enables **fractional ownership**. This will increase liquidity in the market, as well as shared accountability and new forms of value creation.

Standards

Standardization is crucial for effective cooperation on a global scale. It ensures a common language and understanding of the subject at hand. Token standards are standardized protocols for representing and exchanging assets or value on a blockchain platform. By implementing token standards, organizations can create and issue tokens that represent specific assets or rights, such as ownership, access, or entitlement, and exchange these tokens in a transparent and secure manner. ERC-20 and ERC-721[10] are examples of standards in blockchain protocols.

Smart Contracts

Smart contracts are self-executing contracts with predefined conditions and actions written in code. These contracts automatically execute and enforce agreements when specific conditions are met. By utilizing smart contracts, parties can automate processes, execute transactions, and enforce rules without the need for intermediaries. This automation streamlines operations, reduces costs, and ensures trust through code-driven execution.

Pull Systems

The concept of a pull system in blockchain refers to the creation of demand or attraction for resources, services, or actions using tokens. Instead of a traditional push system, where resources are allocated based on forecasts or predetermined schedules, a pull system utilizes token incentives to attract resources or actions when needed. This incentivizes participants to provide their services or resources based on real-time demand or requirements within the network. Every time a transaction takes place, it is recorded on the blockchain as a status update. This means there is always an up-to-date status available.

Feedback Loops

Blockchain ecosystems can incorporate feedback loops by allowing participants to provide input, suggestions, or feedback. Every participant can submit blockchain improvement proposals to improve the network. If a majority of votes in the network think that the proposal is a good idea, it can be implemented.

Smart contracts can be programmed to adapt to changing needs based on this feedback. This continuous improvement cycle aligns with Lean principles by fostering a culture of continuous improvement and ensuring that the system evolves to better serve the needs of its users.

In summary, blockchain uses token incentives, token marketing, tokenization, standards, smart contracts, pull systems, and feedback loops to build a decentralized system encouraging good behavior and creating a more efficient flow and exchange of value.

Blockchain adds value to transactional processes across the following five R's (or four R's and an "I"). See Figure 2.4.

Resources

Intellectual property, verifiable credentials, linked data links information to a precise uniform resource identifier (URI). Similar to how a URL points to a specific website, a computer can automatically understand the information received from a URI.

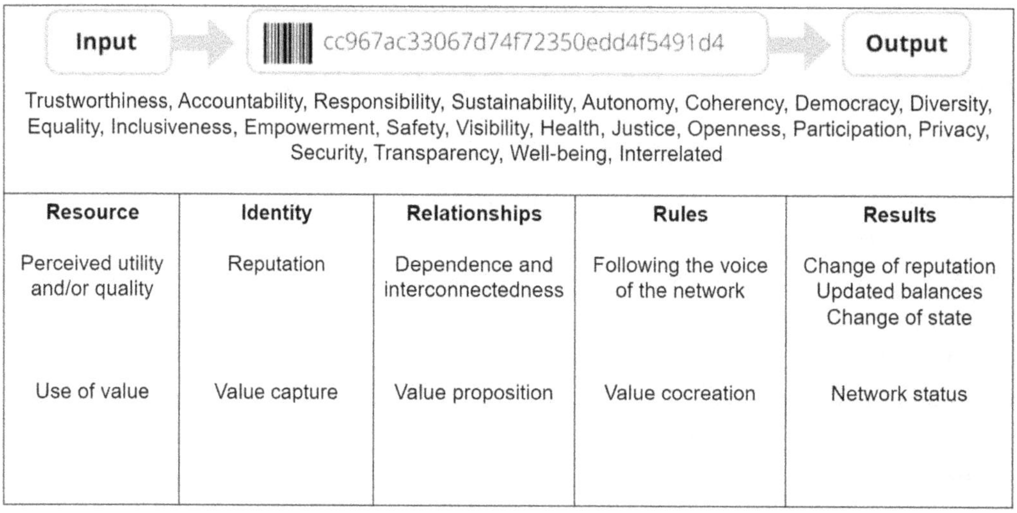

Input →	‖‖‖ cc967ac33067d74f72350edd4f5491d4 →	Output
Trustworthiness, Accountability, Responsibility, Sustainability, Autonomy, Coherency, Democracy, Diversity, Equality, Inclusiveness, Empowerment, Safety, Visibility, Health, Justice, Openness, Participation, Privacy, Security, Transparency, Well-being, Interrelated			

Resource	Identity	Relationships	Rules	Results
Perceived utility and/or quality	Reputation	Dependence and interconnectedness	Following the voice of the network	Change of reputation Updated balances Change of state
Use of value	Value capture	Value proposition	Value cocreation	Network status

Figure 2.4   Blockchain adds value to transactional processes across five areas (4Rs and an I)

Identities (Roles)

Intellectual property management with unique identifiers for people, self-sovereign identities (SSI), for companies (wallets), for content identity (CID), and decentralized identifiers for products (DID). DID's rely on cryptography to prove that you are in control of a given identity.

Relationships

Digital data carriers on physical products (like a QR code or RFID) with a look-up mechanism; legal entity identifier.

Rules

Data processing, data exchange, storage, authentication, integrity, security, and privacy.

Results

Sustainable products regulation, greenhouse gas emissions reporting, etc.

What Is the Added Value of Blockchain Technology?

Let's explore why blockchain is a necessary addition to Lean. We will do this by looking at the six revelations of Russell L. Ackoff:

Blockchain technology addresses several of the concerns highlighted by Ackoff.

The six revelations of Russell L. Ackoff[11]:

1. Improving the performance of the parts of a system taken separately will not necessarily improve the performance of the whole; in fact, it may harm the whole.
2. Problems are not disciplinary in nature but are holistic.
3. The best thing that can be done to a problem is not to solve it but to dissolve it.
4. The healthcare system of the United States is not a healthcare system; it is a sickness-and-disability-care system.

5. The educational system is not dedicated to producing learning by students but teaching by teachers—and teaching is a major obstruction to learning.
6. The principal function of most corporations is not to maximize shareholder value, but to maximize the standard of living of those who manage the corporation.

Holistic Nature of Problems

Blockchain's decentralized and transparent nature allows for a holistic approach to problem-solving. It emphasizes the entire system rather than isolated parts. By maintaining an immutable ledger of transactions across various entities, it provides a comprehensive view, aiding in understanding and solving complex problems within the system.

Problem Dissolution

Ackoff's idea that dissolving a problem is more effective than merely solving it aligns with blockchain's ability to create trust, alignment, accountability, and transparency. By decentralizing control and increasing transparency, blockchain minimizes problems by eliminating the need for intermediaries and reducing fraud or disputes.

Healthcare and Education System Transformations

Blockchain has the potential to transform healthcare and education. In healthcare, it can secure patient records, enhance data sharing among providers, and improve the overall system's efficiency. Regarding education, blockchain-based credentialing systems can validate and securely store academic achievements, transforming the way credentials are verified and shared.

Corporate Function

While Ackoff acknowledges that the main goal of business has historically focused on creating value for business owners, blockchain can now assist in aligning the business goals with broader goals such as the 17 SDGs for global sustainability. Blockchain can also increase accountability and transparency in corporate governance (CSRD, Corporate Sustainability Reporting Directive), reflecting a commitment that goes beyond maximizing shareholder value and takes into account the well-being of all stakeholders and the environment.

In summary, Blockchain technology provides decentralization, transparency, consensus, and immutability which enable solutions to systemic issues in business and society highlighted by Russell Ackoff. This will help to create more effective, efficient, and equitable systems across multiple sectors and industries.

Summary

The chapter introduces blockchain and Web 3, highlighting the paradigm shift in value exchange, enabling machines to autonomously participate in economic activities through smart contracts and token incentives.

We have emphasized how blockchain eliminates system waste, citing its role in removing inefficiencies and waste created by a lack of transparency, collaboration, coordination, and communication. The discussion also includes the impact on trust, SDGs, and specific blockchain initiatives supporting these goals.

A reflection on the externalities of waste in organizational models is presented, posing ethical questions about waste creation and organizational design.

The chapter concludes by exploring how blockchain improves the flow within ecosystems, utilizing token incentives, tokenization, and smart contracts. It also presents a summary of the digitized five R's: Roles, Relationships, Rules, Resources, and Results.

Finally, the chapter addresses the need for Blockchain technology by aligning with the revelations of Russell L. Ackoff. It emphasizes blockchain's holistic approach to problem-solving, its potential to dissolve problems seen in traditional organizational models, and its transformative impact on areas such as healthcare, education and corporate governance. Blockchain technology is at its core a tool for transparent, efficient, and equitable system design.

Lean Blockchain System Thinking = Learn How to See and Design Ecosystem Value

Figure 2.5 shows all the separate components necessary to design an ecosystem of value.

Figure 2.6 shows a scenario in which stakeholders shield their inventory information, preventing visibility of their product quantities and quality.

LEAN HOUSE OF VALUE

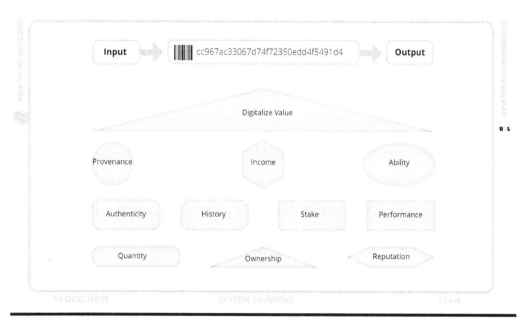

Figure 2.5 The components necessary to design an ecosystem of value.

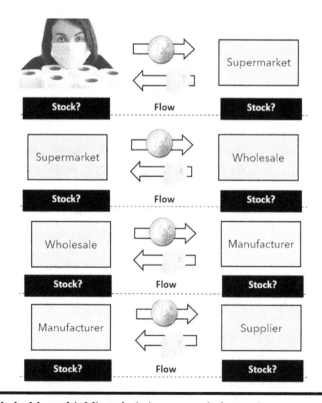

Figure 2.6 Stakeholders shielding their inventory information, preventing visibility of their product quantities and quality.

What is the purpose of this system?

What are the social, financial, and ecological consequences of this organizational model?

A book recommendation is: https://thenetworkstate.com/.

Technology has enabled us to start new companies, new communities, and new currencies. But can we use it to start new cities, or even new countries? This book explains how to build the successor to the nation-state, a concept we call the network state.

Notes

1. Morris, D. Aligning on Purpose, for Value, and in Flow. davidjcmorris.com.
2. Taiichi Ohno's Workplace Management: English Translation 2007, 2009.
3. Gemba. What Does It Mean? https://www.lean.org/lexicon-terms/gemba/.
4. Gemba. What Does It Mean? https://www.lean.org/lexicon-terms/gemba/.
5. Shingo, S. (1987). *The Sayings of Shigeo Shingo: Key Strategies for Plant Improvement.*
6. Hutchins, D. C. (1985). *Quality Circles Handbook.*
7. Deus, H. After God and Man, Algorithms Will Make the Decisions. Yuval Noah Harari (ynharari.com).
8. Senge, P. (2006). *The Fifth Discipline: The Art and Practice of the Learning Organisation.*
9. Ackoff, R. L. (2007). *Systems Thinking for Curious Managers: With 40 New Management F-Laws.*
10. Ethereum Development Standards. ethereum.org.
11. Ackoff, R. L. (2007). *Systems Thinking for Curious Managers: With 40 New Management F-Laws.*

Chapter 3

Balancing

Ecosystem balance is the ability of a community to tolerate disturbances without entering a qualitatively different state. Balance creates stability in the sense of resilience, persistence, and resistance to major change.[1] This requires a transformation from a focus solely on growth and efficiency to ecosystem balancing, in which collective learning, adaptability, flexibility, and collaboration are the success factors.

Balancing is essential for sustainability.

For any system, when the inflow of a resource becomes less than the outflow, then depletion of that resource occurs. An example of this is the overfishing of certain species of fish in our oceans.[2]

Balance is required for sustainability. Any system that does not have balance will ultimately be unsustainable.

This chapter explores the concept of balance and how Lean principles, together with Blockchain technology and Systems Thinking, can improve balance and equilibrium in order to achieve greater system sustainability.

Learning Objectives

Upon completing this chapter, you will be familiar with:

- The concept of balancing a system
- System failure
- Single-entry accounting
- Double-entry accounting

DOI: 10.4324/9781003599715-3

- Trust in third parties
- Triple-entry accounting

Inflows and Outflows

Balancing a system is achieved by controlling the flow of resources, information, and value. It requires precise coordination between system elements to ensure the correct quantities of **inflows** and **outflows**.

Balancing is important for several reasons:

- Efficiency maximization
  By managing **inflows and outflows**, resources are optimized for efficient utilization, reducing both underutilization and overwhelming capacities.

- Stability maintenance
  A balanced system reduces bottlenecks and disruptions, resulting in improved **stability** and consistent performance.

- Resource optimization
  By correctly managing **inflows and outflows**, resources are optimized for efficient utilization, reducing both the waste of overproduction as well as the wastes of excessive inventories and work-in-progress. This requires analyzing the entire system and not just optimizing the parts of the system without taking the whole into account.

- Adaptability/flexibility enhancement
  A balanced system is more adaptable and flexible, allowing rapid response to environmental or unexpected external stresses or demands.

- Quality improvement
  Ensuring that inputs are matched to outputs and focusing on improvements to the whole system (rather than silos within the system) leads to higher quality outputs, which in turn improves overall performance and productivity. This approach enhances the quality of outputs in both manufacturing processes as well as service delivery systems.

■ Continuous improvements
  Balancing provides a foundation for continual improvement by providing a standard for monitoring and adjustments (actions taken when balance is lost).

    In summary, balancing inflows and outflows is critical in process management, improving efficiency, stability, adaptability, quality, and continuous improvement for superior system performance.

What If We Don't Balance the System?

The tragedy of the commons is a well-known system failure (system archetype). It refers to a situation in which individuals, acting in their self-interest, deplete or spoil a shared resource. In the long term, this leads to the degradation or depletion of the resource.

    The metaphor is the title of a 1968 essay by ecologist Garrett Hardin.[3]

> *An example of the tragedy of the commons is overfishing in oceans or seas. Fishermen, acting in their own interest, are willing to catch as many fish as possible to maximize their profits. When multiple fishermen follow this practice without any regulation or cooperation, it can lead to the collapse of the fish stocks, impacting not only the fishermen but also the ecosystem and future availability of fish resources for everyone. This overexploitation occurs because no one owns the fishery, and individual actors prioritize their short-term gains over the long-term health of the resource.*

The 17 sustainable development goals[4] suggested by the United Nations highlight the need for more sustainable, inclusive, and equitable practices. However commendable these goals are, they also raise some important questions:

■ How do we translate these theoretical goals into execution?
■ How do we measure sustainability? What are the metrics used?
■ How do we monitor and control the inflows and outflows of global supply chains?
■ Is there a form of accounting that can be used to track the metrics used to define sustainable goals?
■ Who controls the accounting for meeting sustainable goals?
■ Can we trust the controller of the accounting method?

Within this chapter, we explore new possibilities for answering these questions which are enabled by Blockchain technology.

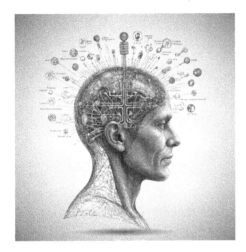

"Life is like accounting; everything must be balanced".
– Unknown

Balancing Tools: Accounting

To better understand the opportunities to improve balancing, we need to better understand the principles **of accounting and its evolution**.
This journey takes us from:

1. The physical ages of stone, bronze and iron with **trust in single-entry accounting**
2. The industrial age with **trust in double-entry accounting**
3. The internet age, double-entry accounting with trust in third parties (that synchronize our balances in separate ledgers)
4. Finally, into the age of the internet of trust (blockchain), **with trust in computer code protocols that provide a decentralized consensus on the truth: triple-entry accounting**

Trust in Single-Entry Accounting

A good way to explain single-entry accounting is to understand the story of Yap Island. Yap Island was a relatively small community (less than 10,000 people*) that had a unique accounting system. It gives us an idea of how the cooperation, coordination, and communication of value transactions were

done in the past. It is the primitive variant of process management: input →
process → output.[5]

*https://miltonfriedman.hoover.org/internal/media/dispatcher/215061

System Methodology: Word of Mouth

On Yap Island, one of the Caroline Islands in Micronesia, during the period
from approximately 1899 to 1919, transactions were carried out using a
system known as "word of mouth". This unique method of exchange was
used due to the impracticality of physically moving massive stone disks
called *Rai Stones*, which served as the island's representation of ownership.

Remi
-10
5
7
4
-12

"You have to understand accounting and you have to understand
the nuances of accounting. It's the language of business and it's an
imperfect language, but unless you are willing to put in the effort to
learn accounting—how to read and interpret financial statements—
you really shouldn't select stocks yourself".
—Warren Buffett

How Does the Word-of-Mouth System Work?

In the Yapese community, everyone was well informed about the property and the unique history behind each stone. This collective knowledge
extended to knowing the specific owner, the location of the stone, and the
story behind its acquisition.

The transfer of ownership of these Rai Stones was a communal affair,
characterized by public expressions in a shared space. When a transfer
occurred, the entire community would gather to witness the exchange.
During these public meetings, the transfer of ownership was announced, and
the name of the new owner was added to the shared memory of the community. The crucial element lay in the collective recognition and acceptance
of this transfer. Once the community recognized the stone's new owner, it
laid the foundation for future transactions. This **consensus and trust** in the
community became the cornerstone for subsequent ownership exchanges.

Essentially, Yap Island's word-of-mouth system relied on the collective
memory of a community. The trust in the truth was based on a shared commitment of the community to maintain the integrity of ownership. It is a
remarkable example of how a society can develop a functioning economic
system based on shared knowledge and trust, **even without physical
money, written documents, or technology like the internet.**

Rai stone at the Hamburg Ethnology Museum: https://en.wikipedia.org/wiki/Rai_stones

What makes "the stone money" of Yap even more remarkable is the method of transaction. Carrying these massive discs was nearly impossible, so the Yapese people devised a unique system of exchange. It wasn't the physical transfer of the stone that determined ownership, but **rather a system of word of mouth and oral history**. Everyone in the community knew who the rightful owner of each stone was, and this collective understanding made the system function seamlessly.

The Rai Stone functioned as **the first technological oracle** because it facilitated communication between community members who could not trust each other 100%.

The function includes:

■ Listening to the needs of the system and knowing their boundaries
■ Collect and broadcast data
■ Make use of a standard process procedure
■ Shows the dependency with others
■ Validate and create consensus of the output

The community supervisor often spoke the truth or made the final judgement when there was uncertainty regarding the decision-making process.

The use of the Rai stones is an example of **single-entry accounting**. Single-entry accounting is a system in which financial transactions are recorded in one account, without a corresponding entry being made in a second account. This system was used in ancient civilizations and was the first recorded accounting method. The stones could be used because there was a basis of trust within the community.

"Capital isn't this pile of money sitting somewhere; it's an accounting construct".
Bethany McLean[6]

Rai Stone at the Hamburg Ethnology Museum, Germany.

Double-Entry Accounting

While the stones effectively facilitated coordination within the community, they failed to address transactions beyond its boundaries. This limitation stemmed from outsiders' lack of recognition regarding the value or significance of these stones. The resolution to this issue emerged with the invention of double-entry accounting, better known as **bookkeeping**.

Figure 3.1   Double-entry bookkeeping has been a standard since the 14th century.

Double-entry accounting is a system in which financial transactions are recorded in two accounts with a corresponding debit and credit entry made in each account. This system was developed in the 14th century by an Italian mathematician[7] and is still in use today. The main advantage of double-entry accounting is that it helps to ensure the accuracy and completeness of financial records by requiring that there be a corresponding entry for every transaction.

The invention of double-entry accounting brought several key benefits compared to single-entry accounting:

Increased Accuracy

Double-entry accounting introduced the practice of recording each financial transaction in two separate accounts, with corresponding debit and credit entries. This system helped ensure that the books of accounts stayed in balance. This balanced approach significantly **reduced errors and improved**

the accuracy of financial records. In single-entry accounting, there is a higher risk of overlooking or misreporting transactions.

Better Financial Control

With double-entry accounting, businesses could more effectively track their financial transactions and account for every change in their financial position. This **improved control and transparency** over their financial activities, making it easier to detect discrepancies, fraud, or irregularities.

Clearer Financial Position

Double-entry accounting provided a more comprehensive view of an organization's financial position. It allowed for the creation of a balance sheet that showed assets, liabilities, and owners' equity, giving **a snapshot of the organization's financial health** at any given time. Single-entry accounting lacks the structure to generate such detailed financial statements.

Enhanced Decision-Making

The ability to generate detailed financial statements and reports from double-entry accounting data empowered businesses and organizations to make **more informed decisions**. They could analyze their financial performance, evaluate profitability, and identify areas for improvement more effectively.

Improved Auditing

Double-entry accounting made it easier for auditors to review and verify financial records. The clear structure of debits and credits and the principle of keeping the books in balance facilitated the auditing process. This was crucial for **building trust** with investors, lenders, and stakeholders.

Scale and Complexity

Double-entry accounting allows for the processing of a larger number of transactions that are scalable across community or country borders. It provides a more comprehensive and widely accepted picture of the financial condition of organizations.

Accrual Accounting

Double-entry accounting forms the basis for accrual accounting, which is essential for matching revenues and expenses in the period they occur. This is particularly important for accurately representing the financial performance of businesses and organizations over time.

In summary, double-entry accounting introduced greater accuracy, control, and transparency into financial record-keeping, making it an indispensable tool for businesses and organizations to manage their finances effectively and make informed decisions. It has become the standard accounting method used by businesses, governments, and organizations around the world.

> "The word accounting comes from the word accountability. If you are going to be rich, you need to be accountable for your money".
> **– Robert Kiyosaki**

Trust in Third Parties

The internet has not revolutionized accounting like double-entry bookkeeping did for single accounting. However, it is crucial to acknowledge how the internet has transformed our trust in organizations.

It has given rise to new organizational and business models, introducing innovative products and seduction techniques.

> While before the internet era we had no need to be reachable by mobile phone, during the internet era we have become completely dependent on mobile phone.

Big Data: The New Currency of the Digital Age

In today's digital landscape, big data reigns supreme, becoming the new currency in the digital economy. Thanks to the pivotal role played by data platforms, they have become treasure troves of customer insights, offering boundless opportunities to captivate and engage. Beyond their efficiency as business models, platforms hold a remarkable advantage: the mastery of big data coordination. This data is not only valuable, it's the cornerstone of an essential new revenue model.

The Internet's Transformative Impact

The internet has ushered in a new era of transformation:

- A radically reimagined organizational structure
- Innovative revenue and deduction models
- Unprecedented analytical possibilities
- New products and insights as a service

As we navigate this wave of progress, pressing questions arise: Are these tech giants handling our data with the respect it deserves? Do we trust these companies with our data? Are our priorities correctly aligned?

Stories about tech companies collecting all our data, creating complex profiles, and using those profiles for seduction and influence have become increasingly common.

Data breaches are also on the rise, which should normally lead to the question: "Why do we put more trust in these tech giants than in our own governments?"

Have we become too dependent on these organizations or addicted?

A Lesson from the Internet: Every Interaction Is a Transaction

Consider the internet, a place where innovation has rewritten the rules. It brought forth social interactions previously unimaginable, like "X", Facebook, LinkedIn, WhatsApp, and Snapchat, redefining how we communicate.

It gave birth to e-commerce, replacing physical stores, and paved the way for self-publishing, leaving print media behind. The arrival of the internet brought new interaction options that proved more effective and efficient than their physical counterparts. In this digital landscape, platforms are the dominant business model of the 21st century. Instead of offering products, they create social networks, shifting our perspective from linear product-oriented thinking to platform-oriented thinking, with an emphasis on coordination and facilitation. The effects of revolutionary technology, such as the internet, often unravel like a compelling tale—clear and evident in hindsight, yet challenging to foresee in advance.

In the past, landowners were in control, with farmers creating value through their work. The majority of this value ended up in the landowner's pockets. In our digital world, the land has been replaced by big data, cleverly harnessed by platform economies (FAANG companies).[8]

The internet is often criticized for treating individuals as commodities, diminishing our control over personal data. Companies utilize this data at the expense of user autonomy, sometimes engaging in actions that conflict with user interests.

Just as with the invention of the wheel and the development of the internet, blockchain brings unforeseen consequences. To stay ahead, embracing change is crucial, alongside recognizing the internet's limitations. Letting go of outdated habits and embracing a new, innovative approach is imperative. This new form of accounting may allow us to work in a more balanced way.

Triple-Entry Accounting

Visualize each interaction as a transaction. See Figure 3.2.

The current Internet protocol (TCP/IP) facilitates information transactions without intermediaries. However, transactions involving tangible value like voting rights, money, or diplomas necessitate intermediaries. These entities manage, monitor, and control access to information, often charging fees. Examples include government bodies, banks, accountants, and educational institutions.

Why are intermediaries necessary? It comes down to **trust**. Monitoring the debit and credit flows of the balance sheet is crucial. If everyone were to maintain their own balance sheet, trust in the data would be compromised. Therefore, the existence of structured trust within specific roles, organizations, and supervisors becomes trustless.

LEAN VALUE FLOW

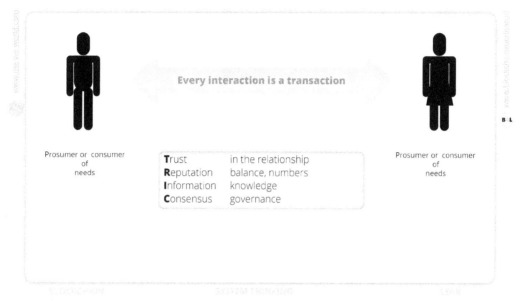

Every interaction is a transaction

Prosumer or consumer
of
needs

Trust   in the relationship
Reputation   balance, numbers
Information   knowledge
Consensus   governance

Prosumer or consumer
of
needs

Figure 3.2 Every interaction is a transaction.

Blockchain promises to redefine this landscape, offering a vision where trust and transactions flourish in a more open, decentralized, secure, and transparent way. It's a game-changer with the potential to reshape the way we interact and **balance our inflows and outflows of value**.

In the traditional setup, customers are beholden to the opening hours and service availability of intermediaries, which primarily exist to safeguard the integrity of transactions and prevent duplicity or fraud. The data they handle is pivotal, serving as a signal of the "status" in legal, social, or personal contexts.

From the Lean perspective, **these intermediaries** can be viewed as **the largest obstacles** in the flow of value. They create waiting times, necessitate transport, and complicate the movement of people and goods. What if we could chart a different course?

The Rise of Triple Accounting

Blockchain technology emerges as a **digital intermediary**, a disruptor in the science of transaction record-keeping and distribution across a decentralized network. Every participant in this network can verify transaction statuses at any moment, providing irrefutable evidence of their occurrence.

LEAN ACCOUNTING

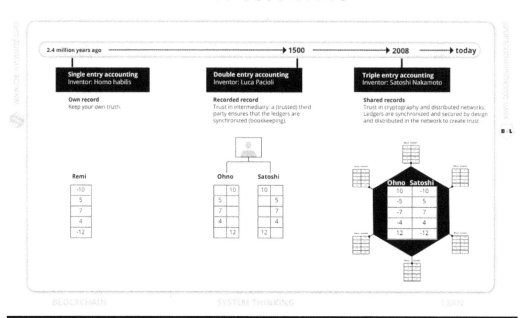

Figure 3.3   The move over time from single entry accounting to double entry accounting to triple entry accounting.

This groundbreaking feature, enabling proof without reliance on intermediaries, ushers in a revolutionary approach to organization.

When information resides in a single central location, it becomes a vulnerable point of failure, susceptible to manipulation and unauthorized access. Blockchain, however, shatters this paradigm, eliminating the single point of failure and fortifying data integrity against tampering.

We have also created a more "Lean" accounting system as we moved through the ages from single- to double-, and finally to triple-entry accounting. See Figure 3.3.

Summary

The chapter begins by highlighting the critical importance of balancing in **Lean System Thinking**. Maintaining balance in a system involves regulating the flow of resources, ensuring efficiency, stability, adaptability, quality, and continuous improvement. Failure to balance a system leads to the tragedy of the commons, where self-interest depletes shared resources, as seen in overfishing.

The discussion progresses through historical accounting methods: single-entry accounting, exemplified by Yap Island's word-of-mouth system, and the evolution to double-entry accounting. Double-entry accounting brought accuracy, financial control, and transparency to record-keeping.

The narrative shifts to the impact of the internet age, exploring the necessity of trust in third parties for transactions involving tangible value. It emphasizes big data's role as a dominant currency in the digital age and questions the trustworthiness of centralized private companies and governments with our data.

The emergence of Blockchain technology is presented as a potential solution for trust and transparency issues, leading to the concept of triple-entry accounting. Blockchain promises decentralization, security, and transparency, potentially revolutionizing interactions by minimizing reliance on intermediaries.

Lastly, the convergence of Lean philosophy and Blockchain technology is explored. Lean philosophy's focus on optimizing value streams meets blockchain's potential for disintermediation, reshaping traditional organizational structures and **balancing the whole system**. See Figure 3.4.

Overall, the chapter provides a holistic perspective on the importance of balancing systems, the evolution of accounting principles, and the transformative potential of Blockchain technology in revolutionizing trust and transparency in transactions.

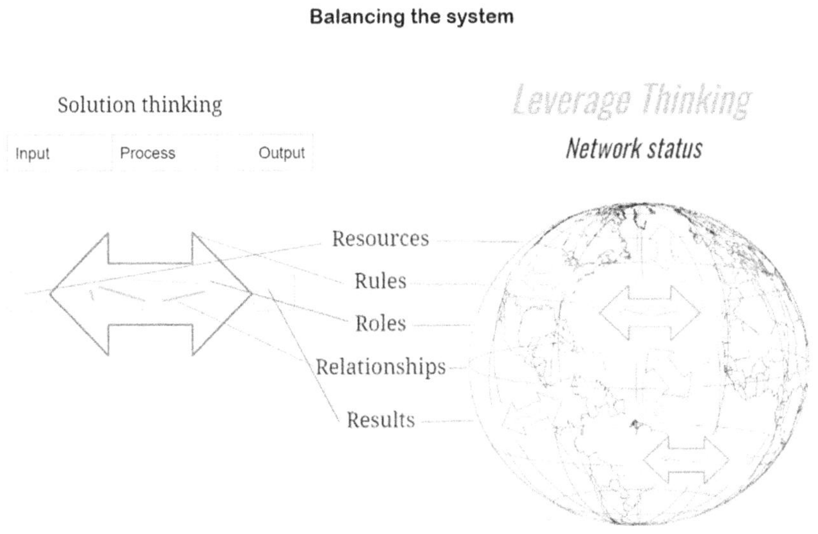

Figure 3.4 Bockchain's potential for reshaping traditional organizational structures and balancing the whole system.

Blockchain technology offers a means of organizing value flows by providing a decentralized, immutable, and transparent platform for exchanging assets and information. While money is certainly a form of value exchange, blockchain extends beyond currency transactions and encompasses a wide range of assets and rights, making it a versatile tool for organizing and facilitating value flows in various domains.

Here is an example of an initiative using triple accounting on Blockchain technology.

Regen Network and "Eco Credits"

Regen Network is a blockchain-based project focused on regenerative activities.[9] Regen Network has chosen to use the term "Eco credit". This blog gives an overview of "eco credits", the history of its use within the Regen Network community, and some of the alternatives that have been considered. What is important is that we are using a term that is unambiguous in the aim of the agreement between counter parties.

- Asset-based accounting
- Value-based accounting
- Contribution-based accounting
- Carbon offset and mitigation-based accounting
- Carbon removal-based crediting
- Payment for results
- Environmental stewardship payments
- Ecological benefit accounting and payments
- Ecosystem service accounting and payments

2.1 Ecological Protocol Frameworks

Regen Ledger provides three core ecological protocol frameworks:

- Ecological State Protocols (ESPs) define the algorithms and conditions necessary to verify a certain state or change of state on a piece of land

- Ecological Contracts (ECs) allow us to fund and reward desired change in ecological state

- Supply Protocols (SPs) allow us to tie ecological state into supply chains in trusted ways

Notes

1. Pimm, S. L. (1992). The Balance of Nature?: Ecological Issues in the Conservation of Species and Communities.
2. What is Overfishing? Facts, Effects and Overfishing Solutions. https://www .worldwildlife.org/threats/overfishing.
3. Hardin, G. (1968). The Tragedy of the Commons. *Science,* 162(3859), 1243–1248. doi:10.1126/science.162.3859.1243.
4. THE 17 GOALS. Sustainable Development. https://sdgs.un.org/g.
5. Friedman, M. The Island of Stone Money. https://miltonfriedman.hoover.org/ internal/media/dispatcher/215061.
6. McLean, B. (2024). *The Smartest Guys in the Room: The Amazing Rise and Scandalous Fall of Enron.*
7. Double-entry bookkeeping (DEB) was probably developed in business practice as early as the thirteenth century, but was first published in 1494 as a system by the Italian mathematician Luca Pacioli: Diwan, J. *Accounting Concepts & Theories.* London: Morre. pp. 001–002. id# 94452.
8. FAANG: Facebook (now called 'Meta'), Amazon, Apple, Netflix, Google.
9. The Degen Network. https://medium.com/regen-network/to-credit-or-not-to -credit-de48ba7da8c4.

Chapter 4

Cause and Effect

Learning Objectives

Upon completing this chapter, you will be familiar with:

- Cause-and-effect relationships
- The Fishbone Diagram
- The creation of "Waste by design"
- The five basic concepts for Lean System Thinkers
- The importance of understanding the end-to-end process
- Critical Success Factors (CSFs)
- The Voice(s) of the Network (VoN)
- Three stream value flow framework
- Learning to analyze the whole (rather than the parts)
- Explanation of a "Black Box" design
- Cause and effect for system thinkers!
- The Iceberg model for cause and effect

Introduction

Imagine you have a company that manufactures and sells products. You have a production line with various steps, such as manufacturing components, assembling the final product, packaging, and shipment. You decide to implement a process mining tool to try to improve the efficiency of your

DOI: 10.4324/9781003599715-4

production line. The idea is to identify and optimize bottlenecks and inefficiencies within the process.

By implementing process mining, you may be able to identify where inefficiencies within your process are occurring, but it doesn't necessarily identify the root cause of the problem.

It would not, for example, be able to identify if the wrong information or incomplete information is being supplied as inputs to the process. This information is outside of the scope of the process mining tool, and we are often unable to validate the accuracy of that information.

This is similar to a doctor only identifying the symptoms of a disease (high temperature, fatigue, headaches, etc.) without understanding the underlying cause of the disease and even how it was transmitted.

A more holistic, system-wide approach not only identifies symptoms within a process but also understands the root causes of the symptoms which are originating from outside of the process.

This is an excellent use of Blockchain technology, where information can be shared more transparently and directly among all parties involved in a supply chain or any extended value-chain.

Blockchain technology achieves this by providing one common ledger of data transactions, with data integrity and security "by-design" which can be trusted by all parties (stakeholders).

Blockchain technology creates the ability to allow access only to the specific information needed by specific parties to be efficient and effective in the part of the value chain that they control. Blockchain also securely protects (by-design) information (such as internal financial records or personal information) from those parties who have no good reason to access it.

Rules are assigned to specific data categories and to specific stakeholder identities (digital identities) to define access rights throughout the supply chain or value-chain.

Cause and Effect

Cause and effect describes the relationship between two events or actions when one event or action influences another event or action. For example, reducing body temperature to below 35°C can cause death (the effect). See Figure 4.1.

Cause-and-effect relationships can have multiple levels of complexity. For example, the reduction in body temperature to below 35 degrees *causes* the

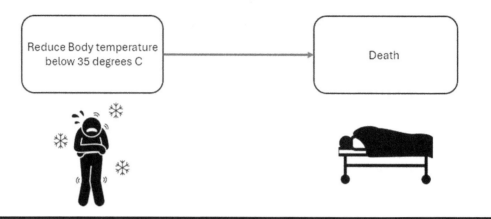

Figure 4.1 Simple example of cause and effect.

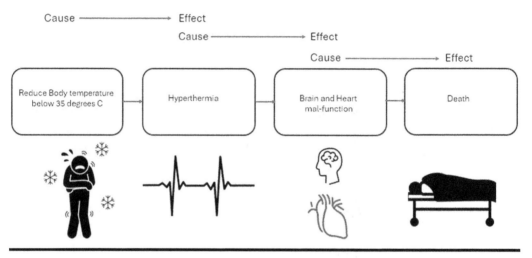

Figure 4.2 A cause-and-effect chain.

physiological condition called hypothermia. Hypothermia *causes* various neurological changes in the body which causes brain and heart function to deteriorate which finally *causes* death. See Figure 4.2.

Another common way to represent this "Cause-and-effect chain" is to use the **Ishikawa diagram**, commonly referred to as the "**Cause-and-Effect Diagram**" or the "**Fishbone Diagram**". See Figure 4.3.

It is commonly used by practitioners of Lean and Six Sigma as one tool in the DMAIC framework for problem-solving (see Chapter 10: DMAIC).

Can you see why it is called the "Fishbone Diagram"?

Can you think of other causes of death that are not related to the reduction in body temperature? Could you fill in the boxes of the Fishbone Diagram in Figure 4.3 for other potential causes of death?

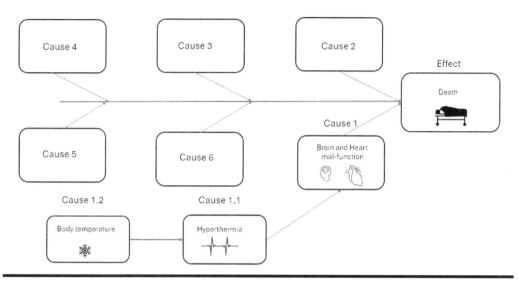

Figure 4.3   An Ishikawa cause-and-effect diagram often called "Fishbone Diagram".

How about:

- Poisoning
- Drowning
- Suffocation
- Drug overdose
- Heart attack
- Loss of blood

Shown in Figure 4.4 is the general form of an **Ishikawa/Cause and Effect/Fishbone Diagram** (you choose which name you like best!).

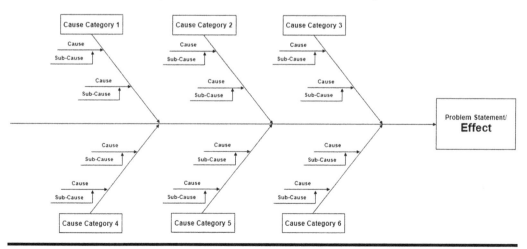

Figure 4.4   General form of Fishbone Diagram made with SigmaXL.

We have used a tool called SigmaXL for this example (see SigmaXL.com).

Cause and Effect in Business Processes

Often the desired outcomes and outputs of a process don't meet the expectations of the process stakeholders, especially the customers of the process.

The customers are experiencing the effects of the process. This is also referred to as "the problem" or "problem statement" for a process.

There are several categories of suggested possible *causes* of problems with the outcomes or outputs of processes. These are often used as a starting point in root-cause analysis using the Fishbone Diagram. These categories of causes have been defined in such a way so that all the words start with the letter "M" and hence they are sometimes referred to as "the 6Ms".

Manpower: Refers to the human resources involved in the process, including their skills, training, and experience

Methods: Describes the procedures, techniques, and processes used to complete tasks within the process

Machines: Includes the equipment, tools, and technology used in the process

Materials: Covers the raw materials, components, and supplies used in the process

Measurements: Involves the metrics, (Key Performance Indicators (KPIs), and data used to evaluate the performance of the process

Mother Nature (Environment): Considers the environmental factors that may impact the process, such as temperature, humidity, or other natural conditions

These 6Ms help in identifying potential causes of problems or inefficiencies within a process.

Cause and Effect in Lean Blockchain

In the context of Lean Blockchain we will explain the following examples of Cause-and-effect relationships:

Causes: A competitive organizational design leads to waste by design

Effect: Increased costs for society

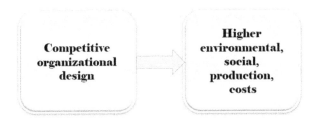

Figure 4.5   Cause and effect in a lean blockchain use-case.

See Figure 4.5.

In this example, inefficient production processes (Methods in the 6Ms) and excessive use of raw materials (Materials in the 6Ms) are identified as the main causes.

The argument goes that this leads to increased waste production and higher environmental and production costs, which are the resulting effects.

However, it is likely that deeper underlying root-causes exist that contribute to these two high-level causes.

This chapter aims to delve into our existing organizational model to uncover the fundamental causes that generate waste, increased costs, and negative effects for society.

See the Fishbone Diagram for high environmental, social, and production costs (Figure 4.6).

To show the relationship between the advantages of Blockchain technology to reduce costs to society, we propose the Ishikawa (Fishbone) Diagram shown in Figure 4.7.

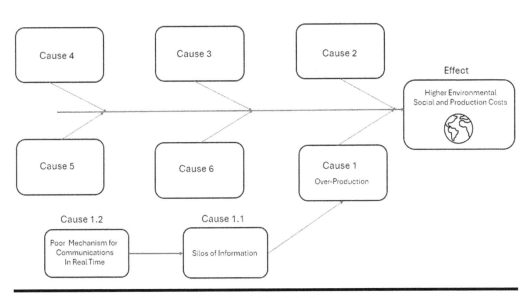

Figure 4.6   Fishbone Diagram for a Lean blockchain use-case.

BLOCKCHAIN ISHIKAWA

Transparency   Efficiency

Transparency is one of the most powerful elements to assure that an activity is done the first-time-right and just-in-time.

Standardization   Lower costs

A standard procedure (SOP) is called a smart contract. A smart contract brings standardization and automation in B-to-B process collaboration.

Plan   **Do**

System
Management
Incentives
Product/service
Skills
Process
Environment
Method

Distributed   Settlement time

Transactions are shared in the network (distributed) and synchronized with coalition partners.

Integrate trust   Risk

Transactions added to the blockchain are inmutable. This ensures data integrity, enables lifecycle preservation and facilitates in a more skin in the game process design.

Act   **Check**

BLOCKCHAIN   SYSTEM THINKING   LEAN

Figure 4.7 How can Blockchain technology have a positive effect for reducing costs to society?

We will now explain this further using a practical health care process example.

"If all you have is a hammer, every problem is a nail".
– Abraham Maslow[1]

Also known as the "law of instrument" or Maslow's Hammer.

Health Care Example for Lean Blockchain Cause and Effect

Understanding the potential of Blockchain technology remains a challenge for many due to its complex nature. Currently too much attention is focused on technical aspects such as decentralization and immutability, or solely on digital currency applications. Our attention is focused on a new process design that organizes the "value" flows in ways previously unthinkable.

 Blockchain is often considered and discussed as a technical innovation. When we look deeper into the concept, we find that it is 90% a process design innovation which also affects the policy, governance, and design rules of any system.

To explain this new organizational structure, we will investigate the completion of a maternity care process. Our goal is to simplify the understanding by breaking down this basic use case and showing how Blockchain can revolutionize process management. So let's start with framing the case study.

Brief Explanation of This Care Process

A patient is insured with the insurer and receives "care credits". After the care is provided, the care provider records the provided care on a worksheet. The worksheet is then forwarded to the care agency for system recording. The data is then transmitted to the insurer, who also enters the same data into their systems. Finalization or settlement is achieved once all information is processed and synchronized.

Our small-scale healthcare scenario involves four primary stakeholders (see Figure 4.8):

- ☑ the patient
- ☑ the insurer
- ☑ the healthcare agency
- ☑ maternity care worker

The process is explained in four simple steps:

1. Customer eligibility approval
   The insurer approves the customer through a know-your-customer (KYC) process, allowing eligibility for care services. Care can be provided only after the customer has been accepted by the insurer.
2. Care provision and documentation
   After care is provided, the maternity care worker generates a timesheet upon the hours care provided. The patient must also sign this for confirmation.

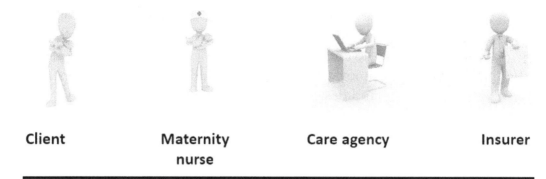

| Client | Maternity nurse | Care agency | Insurer |

Figure 4.8 Healthcare scenario involving four primary stakeholders.

3. Data processing

   The care worker hands over this timesheet to her care agency. The care agency inputs this information into its administration system. An administrative employee of the care agency forwards the information to the insurer.

4. Data synchronization and payment

   The insurer re-enters this data into its administration. This entire process of forwarding and processing information takes about 90 days. Only after 90 days will the care agency pay the worker.

Note: The time at which payments can be made depends on the time at which all parties have the same information and agree on it. Information synchronization is therefore a very crucial element for effective collaboration. The purpose of synchronization is to achieve consistency, accuracy, and reliability of information; a shared reality.

Also note that, in this example, the source information is not shared. Information is continuously duplicated, taken over and over again from a downstream stakeholder.

Within Lean this is called a *push system design*.

Let's deep dive further into this process and explore the main purpose of the whole process and how stakeholders contribute to it. We will do this by learning about the five basic concepts for Lean System Thinkers.

The Five Basic Concepts for Lean System Thinkers (see Figure 4.9) are:

1. The purpose
2. Critical success factors

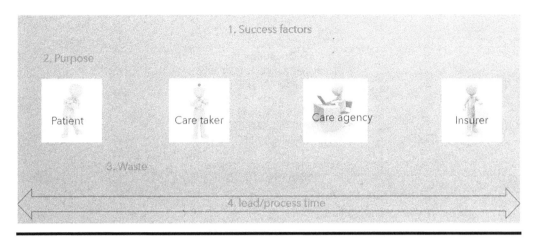

Figure 4.9   The Five Basic Concepts for Lean System Thinkers.

3. Voices of the network
4. Three Flow's settlement
5. Analyze and improve the whole

1. The Purpose

It is critical to recognize that each stakeholder within any system has his or her unique perspectives and objectives. However, when we zoom out to look at the overall purpose of the entire process, we see a variety of relationships, value-driven activities, and joint contributions towards a common goal.

Enter Lean Systems Thinking

Imagine this healthcare process through the lens of a Lean System Thinker. Its core purpose is to ensure the efficient delivery of high-quality healthcare services at optimized costs. To achieve this, the process design must promote optimal collaboration, coordination, and communication (3 C's), striking a balance between cost-effectiveness and quality.

We have observed that the administrative burden associated with synchronizing information has a significant impact on the whole process settlement, hindering its ultimate purpose.

This raises some questions. See Figure 4.10.

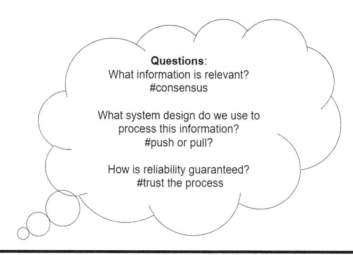

Figure 4.10 Questions that must be answered when designing any information system.

2. Critical Success Factors

In Lean methodology, the CSFs are the pivotal elements crucial for the effectiveness and efficiency of a process or system. By integrating these success factors, organizations can effectively implement Lean principles and realize sustainable improvements in efficiency, quality, and customer satisfaction.

To keep the analysis of this process simple, we have chosen five CSFs that are important in every process. See Figure 4.11.

☑ **Quality**
   Quality is a fundamental success factor in every process. It emphasizes delivering products or services that meet or exceed customer needs and expectations. It involves striving for perfection with **transparency**, **accountability**, effective resource management, and ensuring consistency in output. Functionality and features which work as expected and accuracy of information are examples of quality CSFs.

☑ **Reliability**
   Reliability focuses on the consistency and predictability of processes. It's about creating systems and workflows **you can trust** to produce the expected results consistently, without unexpected errors or variations. The use of **standards** plays an important role in reliability.

☑ **Flexibility**
   Flexibility refers to the ability of a system or process to adapt to changes, variations, or evolving customer needs without compromising efficiency. Lean aims to create flexible systems that can adjust swiftly to market demands or alterations in requirements. **Feedback loops**,

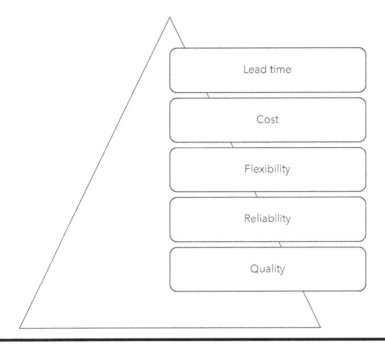

Figure 4.11 **The five most important critical success factors (CSFs).**

> **system analysis**, and **iterative agile improvement methods** are relevant to improving flexibility.

☑ **Cost**

> Cost reduction is a significant CSF of many Lean transformations. It involves identifying and eliminating waste to streamline processes and minimize unnecessary expenses while maintaining or improving quality. Lean strives to achieve cost-effectiveness by **optimizing resource utilization**.

☑ **Lead Time**

> Lead time represents the period from the beginning to the completion of a process. It includes the duration from order placement to delivery (for example, a settlement period of 90 days for paying an invoice). Lean methodology focuses on minimizing lead times by **eliminating non-value-adding tasks (waste)** and limiting **process variations (standardized work)**.

To achieve these CSFs, it is necessary to understand the various objectives of stakeholders and align them with the overall objectives of the end-to-end process.

Our observation shows that current collaboration lacks a comprehensive focus on process optimization. The predominant emphasis is mainly on the objectives of individual stakeholders and their unique capabilities, neglecting their interdependence. This is a *push* strategy which lacks extensive coordination or optimization of the entire workflow.

It is clear that promoting better collaboration, coordination, and communication throughout the end-to-end process—and not just improving individual steps or activities—is crucial for sustainable progress and overall performance improvement.

To achieve this, understanding the objectives, the value-added activities, and specific needs of each stakeholder for the entire process is critical.

We need to make the goals and interests of each stakeholder visible, as well as the goals of the whole ecosystem. Therefore, we introduce the concept of **VoN.**

3. The Voice of the Network

In our maternity healthcare example, each stakeholder has their own set of priorities, expectations, and motivations; we call them "voices". Balancing and aligning these voices is essential for optimizing the total system.

Only then:

- ☑ Care providers can deliver quality services efficiently,
- ☑ Insurers can manage risks and costs effectively,
- ☑ Care agencies can coordinate services optimally,
- ☑ Patients can receive the best possible care with convenience and affordability.

Below is an overview of the goals, the value, and interests of the various stakeholders:

Stakeholders	Value	Voices
Caretaker	Provide care	More time and care for the customer, as little administration as possible, timely payment of wages
Care agency	Facilitate and coordinate care	Short lead time, good quality of care, doing more in the same time
Insurer	Hedging risk	More profit, lower costs, positive image
Patiënt	Receive good care	Good service, low costs, friendly treatment

In the field of Lean methodologies, "the voice of the business", "the voice of the employee", or "the voice of the environment" typically emphasizes optimization from a single or linear perspective.

However, what we really need is a more holistic view that recognizes and aligns multiple voices simultaneously and brings consensus on the diverse needs and goals.

To address this, we introduce the term VON. The VON emphasizes the overall intent of the process, which is to promote support and solidarity for our goals while providing enhanced analytical capabilities.

To strengthen the whole, awareness of three information flows is required. Only when these flows are synchronized, the entire system is considered as fully optimized.

4. The PIP Value Flow Framework

Three Flows Settlement

The stakeholder analysis and "voices" offer us insight into the goals and interests of each stakeholder. Now it is important to think of a strategy in which every stakeholder contributes to the intention of the entire process. We suggest doing this by thinking in three different flows. See Figure 4.12.

- ★ (1) **P**roduct flow,
- ★ (2) **I**nformation transfer, and
- ★ (3) **P**ayment processes are visualized as three distinct flows.

Adopting the strategy of creating and thinking in three different flows proves to be especially useful in identifying constraints that affect settlement time. The goal is to synchronize these three flows as closely as possible,

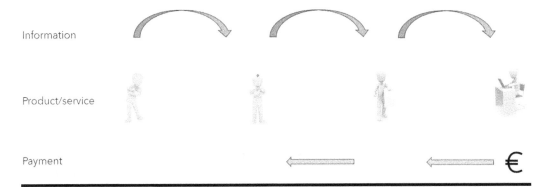

Figure 4.12 The Three Flow's settlement.

aiming to eventually establish a seamless **one-piece flow,** also called **single-piece flow.**[2]

Notice how the information is pushed through the system. From the care provider toward the client, from the caretaker toward the care agency, and finally from the care agency towards the insurer.

Only after every stakeholder has received this information can payment be made.

What would a Single-Piece-Flow look like?

1. When the service has been delivered and approved by the customer
2. The information is immediately synchronized
3. So that the payment can take place

We are looking for a *pull* strategy that ensures that information is immediately synchronized when the customer agrees with the care provided. It is also clear that this is not the case in our current organizational model.

Let us take a closer look at the entire process and try to determine the root causes.

5. Analyze the Whole

When stakeholders don't synchronize their information promptly, it leads to the accumulation of different types of waste, causing significant reductions in efficiency and productivity. Let us look at the specific types of waste that result from our current organizational model.

Waiting Times

Insufficient collaboration frequently causes delays and waiting periods between process steps. For example, when one stakeholder finishes their task, but the subsequent stakeholder isn't promptly ready or informed, it leads to waiting times, wasting resources, and increased inefficiencies.

Over-Processing

When stakeholders operate in silos, the transfer of information between them becomes fragmented and more complicated (consider your email communications). Information may need to be passed through multiple channels, systems, applications, or individuals, which can lead to errors, delays, and the risk of miscommunication.

Multiple/Repeated Data Entry

Inefficient collaboration can result in repeated or redundant data entry. For example, if information is not shared seamlessly between systems or departments, stakeholders might need to manually re-enter data, which is time-consuming and prone to errors.

Reports and Updates

Lack of real-time information sharing can lead to excessive reliance on manual updates and reports to convey critical information. This creates waste in terms of time, resources, and environmental impact.

Errors and Mistakes

When effective collaboration is lacking, errors frequently arise and require correction further along the process. These errors and mistakes might result from miscommunication or a lack of shared understanding among stakeholders, leading to the need for extra time and effort to fix them.

Underutilization of Worker Skills, Ideas, and Talent

How often do we see that talent and new ideas are not utilized because they are busy with administrative work resulting from a lack of coordination? Isn't time spent managing our email a good example of this? Time spent on emails in many cases drains creativity and use of business skills for true value-added work.

When stakeholders fail to align their efforts towards shared goals, it results in inefficiencies, redundancies, and errors within the workflow. Collaborative efforts are pivotal in Lean methodology to minimize these wastes by ensuring seamless communication, shared responsibilities, and collective problem-solving.

Our existing competitive organizational model is **a "black box"** in which we are only aware of our experiences and behaviors within the box and unaware of the root causes or what happens outside of the box.

The lack of alignment and incentives for information sharing within this model inherently leads to waste by design.

See Figure 4.13 below:

	The maternity nurse writes time sheets that they have to sign by the parents.		Printing time sheets, transporting time sheets, stocking time sheets, movement of people
	The maternity care agency receives the time sheets and processes them in its ERP system		Overproduction: retyping information, auditing/controlling information
	The maternity care agency forwards the information to the insurer. The insurer processes this information in its ERP system		Over-processing: duplicating/synchronizing information in different systems
	After 90 days, the maternity care bureau receives its money from the insurer.		Waiting for information. Waiting for the payment. Talent underutilized
	The maternity care agency pays the maternity care provider's salary		Chance of errors when retyping/transporting information

Figure 4.13 Lack of alignment and incentives for information sharing leads to waste by design.

Note: There is always one party not involved in the process. To inform this party about the transaction that has taken place, we currently push information through the system. This approach results in various non-value-adding activities, which we identify as waste in Lean methodology. To optimize the process and reduce waste, we should streamline communication and ensure that information is accessible in real-time without redundant steps.

Cause and Effect for System Thinkers!

With a clearer understanding of the causes of waste, we can apply this cause-and-effect analysis to systemic thinking on a more holistic level using the Causal layered analysis (CLA) framework.

Causal layered analysis is a framework developed by Sohail Inayatullah. The model helps understanding of issues and creating new futures.

The four levels in CLA are represented in the "Iceberg model" as shown in Figure 4.14:

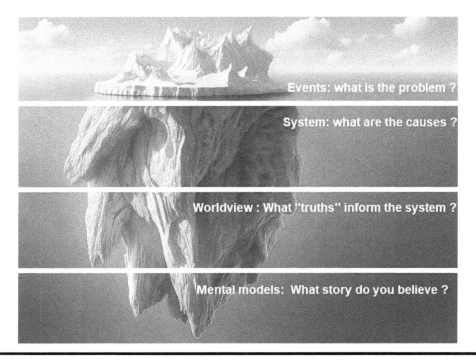

Figure 4.14   The four levels in Causal Layer Analysis (CLA) are represented in the Iceberg model.

Events Level

The surface level is where issues are frequently discussed, encompassing everyday events, facts, and problems highlighted in our news feeds. These are the more obvious and visible problems, addressing the question: "What's happening?" Emergence?

System Level

The system level delves deeper into the structural and systemic causes behind the issues. It examines the underlying social, economic, and political factors contributing to the problems. This level seeks to identify and understand the systems archetypes at play.

Worldview Level

Here, CLA examines the cultural narratives, ideologies, and belief systems that shape how we perceive and interpret the issues. How do we convert information into knowledge? What are the dominant ideologies that support and create the system? What are the paradigms and assumptions that under-lie society?

Mental Models

At the deepest level, CLA examines the collective unconscious and deeply held cultural myths and metaphors that influence our understanding of real-ity. This level involves exploring the symbolic and metaphorical dimensions of issues.

By analyzing issues through these multiple layers, CLA helps uncover deeper insights and facilitates the development of more holistic and trans-formative strategies for addressing challenges and envisioning alternative futures.

Let's apply CLA to better understand the various aspects of Lean systems thinking within a more decentralized system design.

The Event Level (Surface)

The United Nations Sustainable Development Goals reflect and seek to respond to a wide range of issues and challenges facing our world. These goals aim to address global issues related to poverty, inequality, climate change, environmental sustainability, education, health, and more. See Figure 4.15.

What we have learned is that we cannot solve these problems by improv-ing our current organizational structure with continuous improvements (Kaizen). Improving the current organizational structure can lead to effi-ciency but does not make the (competitive) system design more effective. We will therefore have to look for interventions in the system.

The System Level

Here we take a closer look at the systemic factors that contribute to these problems. This includes competitive system design, economic incentives as the main motivation for doing things, regulatory frameworks, preference for ex post control rather than ex ante trust, and centralized governance. For comprehensive system improvement, we recommend using Meadows' 12 leverage points.

We could analyze how existing power structures in sectors such as finance and supply chain management influence the adoption of

Figure 4.15   The 17 Sustainable Development Goals of the United Nations.

decentralized models. In this way, deep-rooted interests in traditional financial systems can resist the disruption brought about by Blockchain technology.

Worldviews (Cultural Level)

This level involves understanding the cultural narratives and ideologies that shape perceptions. It includes examining how different stakeholders work together, trust each other, and improve collaboration, communication, and coordination. If "making money" is the main goal, what are the consequences for society as a whole?

We could explore how different worldviews, such as libertarian ideals of decentralization versus institutional trust, causes externalities, system failures. Additionally, we might consider how media portrayals and public discourse shape public perception of these worldviews.

The Mental Models

At the deepest level, we consider the underlying myths, metaphors, and influences of the collective unconscious. We can explore metaphors such as "the blockchain as a digital ledger of truth" or "decentralization as a democratizing force" to analyze and understand cultural myths around trust, security, and value exchange in the digital age.

By examining problems through multiple lenses, we can develop a more nuanced understanding and identify strategies for broader interventions.

Summary

This chapter underscores the significance of comprehending the **root cause** of waste and inefficiency, identifying the competitive organizational model as a key factor leading to all kinds of waste and externalities when business is transacted between multiple stakeholders trying to achieve different goals.

To optimize and improve the current state in which competitive organizational design with low synchronization of products, information, and payments leads to waste and higher costs for society, we identify the following improvement opportunities:

1. Collaborative System Design

Encourage a shift from purely competitive organizational structures to a more collaborative design. Start with defining the intention and objectives of the end-to-end process, creating a collaborative value stream mapping of the cross-functional teams, departments, entities, and government working together to optimize processes and reduce waste collectively.

By utilizing the "Voice of the Network" concept and aligning stakeholder needs with the end goal through collaborative value stream mapping, organizations can effectively transition towards a more collaborative and purpose-driven approach, thereby optimizing processes and reducing waste collectively.

2. Three Flow Thinking

We have seen that it is crucial that the flow of information between stakeholders is smooth. The CSFs, elements of success—quality, reliability, flexibility, costs, and lead time—depend on the uninterrupted exchange of information. In Lean methodologies, being inclusive is crucial to achieving effectiveness.

The "Three Flow Thinking" method of product, information, and payment is a necessary step for the synchronization and optimization of any processes.

Examine the process in terms of its three value-flows: product flow, information flow, and payment flow.

- Remove activities that do not add value in each of the three flows
- Identify and remove bottlenecks in each of the three flows
- Synchronize the timing of the three flows so that they move in lock-step

3. Invest in Technology and Innovation

Discover technology solutions that can streamline operations and minimize waste. This may involve the adoption of automation, Blockchain technology, and AI-driven analytics for better resource allocation and predictive models to anticipate inefficiencies.

The concept of Lean emerged at a time when the Internet did not yet exist.

As the Internet evolved from Web 1 (read only) to Web 2 (read and write) and e-commerce, each phase has revolutionized the way we approach lean management and information sharing.

Now, with the advent of blockchain and Web 3, the landscape is offering particularly intriguing opportunities for Lean practitioners, as it provides the foundational elements for transformation into fairer, more transparent, more sustainable, and more value-oriented systems.

4. Regulatory Compliance

Donella Meadows[3] described the most important leverage points to intervene in a system.

The distribution of power, the objectives, the culture and incentives of the system are the four most important leverage points.

Power: Compliant with ESG Standards
The controlling powers in the system ensure strict compliance with legal, environmental, and social regulations and standards to reduce the harmful impact of waste on society.

This has typically been a role of the sovereign governments of different countries; however, international treaties and agreements are also exerting regulatory power over individual oganizations.

Rules relating to Environmental, Social, Governance (ESG) together with Corporate, Social Responsibility (CSR) have been recent attempts to exert power over organizations to change behaviors and also provide the data and metrics essential for informing decision-making for both companies and investors.

Objectives: Addressing organizational design flaws
Recognize and proactively address the deficiencies within our current organizational structure and process

Culture: Promoting accountability and transparency
Promote a culture of transparency and accountability to ensure that individuals, organizations, or ecosystems are held accountable for minimizing waste and associated costs.

Incentives: Incentivizing waste reduction initiatives
Create incentives or rewards to inspire and motivate teams or individuals to generate innovative ideas or implement effective strategies aimed at reducing waste within the organization.

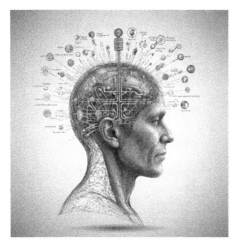

"Show me the incentive and I will show you the outcome". Charlie Mungers
Structuring incentives that induce desired behavior is often more complex than it seems, while misplaced incentives almost always have unintended consequences.

Measure and track progress from a more holistic perspective. Implement KPIs to regularly measure the reduction of waste and associated costs. This data-driven approach will help identify areas that need further improvement.

5. Educate and Raise Awareness

Offer comprehensive training programs for employees, emphasizing the significance of waste reduction and considering consequences impacting society within a system framework.

By integrating these strategies, organizations can transition from a competitive design that generates waste to a more collaborative, efficient, and sustainable model, thereby reducing costs for society as a whole.

Notes

1. Maslow, A. H. (1966). *The Psychology of Science: A Reconnaissance.* Harper & Row.
2. Womack, J. P. and Jones, D. T. (2003). *Lean Thinking Banish Waste and Create Wealth in Your Corporation.* Free Press. Page 60.
3. Donella Hager "Dana" Meadows (March 13, 1941–February 20, 2001) was an American environmental scientist, educator, and writer. She is best known as the lead author of the books *The Limits to Growth* and *Thinking in Systems: A Primer.*

Chapter 5

Principles

"Principles are the basis for developing a vision and value system for all."[1]

– Stephen Covey

Learning Objectives

Upon completing this exploration, you will have a better understanding of:

- Lean principles
- Internet principles
- Blockchain principles
- Systems Thinking principles

Principles provide new perspectives and empower individuals and organizations in unprecedented ways. *Understanding the underlying principles of Lean, Blockchain, and Systems Thinking will elevate our understanding of their combined transformative potential.*

"As to methods, there may be a million and then some, but principles are few. The man who grasps principles can successfully select his own methods. The man who tries methods, ignoring principles, is sure to have trouble".

Harrington Emerson[2]

DOI: 10.4324/9781003599715-5

Lean Principles

Lean is a set of principles, tools, and techniques for balancing both the optimization of resource efficiency (reducing waste in resources) and flow efficiency (the flow of value). Over time, inefficiencies naturally creep into processes, causing waste when seen from the perspective of the **overall customer journey**.

Removing these wasteful elements results in a more streamlined flow in the value stream. The primary focus often revolves around enhancing existing processes.

Lean principles are fundamental concepts that guide process management. Although the philosophy was originally developed in the manufacturing sector, these principles can also be applied to an internet environment or blockchain infrastructure. The core goal remains maximizing value for customers and minimizing waste. The **six principles of Lean** consist of identifying value, mapping the value stream, creating flow, establishing a pull system, striving for perfection, and listening to the stakeholders. Let's have a look at those six principles:

1. **Identifying Value**
   Identify what adds value from the customer's perspective. Focus on understanding the features and attributes for which customers are willing to pay.
2. **Mapping the Value Stream**
   Map out the entire value stream, which includes all the activities required to deliver a product or service to the customer. Identify steps that create value and those that are wasteful or non-value-added.
3. **Creating Flow**
   Streamline the process to achieve a smooth flow of work, minimizing interruptions, delays, and batch processing. This principle seeks to ensure that work moves steadily from one step to the next.
4. **Establishing a Pull System**
   Implement a pull-based system where work is initiated based on customer demand rather than pushing more work into the process. This helps in reducing overproduction and excess inventory.
5. **Perfection with Continuous Improvements**
   Strive for continuous improvement by eliminating waste and relentlessly pursuing excellence. Encourage a culture of learning and innovation to enhance processes continuously.

6. Involve and Listen to the Workers

Involve the community, the network, and the stakeholders in the system in finding the best ideas and coming to a consensus on improvements. Improvement is not only the job of management.

These Lean principles collectively aim to enhance the quality, throughput, the efficiency, and customer satisfaction by focusing on the needs (value) of the customer, minimizing waste, and creating a culture of continuous improvement. See Figure 5.1.

Lean Startup Approach

What we have seen is that the biggest internet companies did not arise from the existing S&P 500 companies. Those new forms of organization followed a Lean Startup methodology using new ways of organizing, business models, and incentives. Could the same be true for Blockchain technology?

The Lean Startup methodology is widely adopted in the startup ecosystem and has proven effective in helping entrepreneurs and businesses build successful products by emphasizing rapid experimentation, customer-centricity, and continuous iteration to achieve product-market fit efficiently.

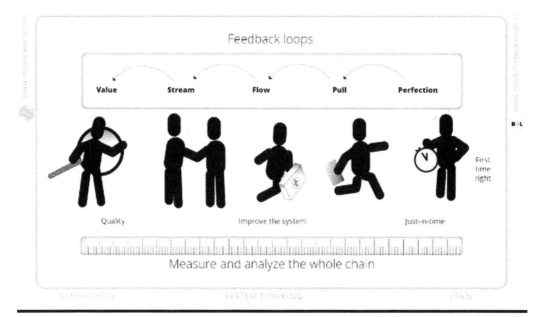

Figure 5.1   Lean principles collectively aim to enhance quality, throughput, efficiency and customer satisfaction by use of feedback loops and creating a culture of continuous improvement.

Internet Principles

By taking a look back at the principles upon which the internet is based, it becomes easier to understand the potential of blockchain.

The internet's foundational principles have revolutionized communication, commerce, and information dissemination. From reshaping social interactions to empowering self-publishing and spawning new business paradigms, the internet has redefined how we interact, transact, and function in the digital sphere.

Moreover, adopting a Lean Startup approach in the internet landscape has birthed some of the most innovative and successful companies. This methodology, emphasizing rapid experimentation and customer-centricity, plays a pivotal role in understanding the internet's transformative power.

1. **Transformation of Social Interaction**
   The internet has introduced entirely new forms of social interaction and platforms such as Facebook, LinkedIn, WhatsApp, Twitter (X), Snapchat, and more. These platforms have revolutionized communication, leading to a decline in traditional methods like post offices and phone booths.

2. **Revolution in E-Commerce**
   The internet has enabled e-commerce, reshaped the retail landscape, and led to the decline of physical stores. Online shopping has become a dominant force in the retail industry.
   Mail order companies first thought they would digitize the stamp, when they later discovered that a new market was emerging for parcel delivery services due to the arrival of web shops. This is an example that shows it is sometimes difficult to see the true transformation before it happens.

3. **Empowerment of Self-Publishing**
   The internet has disrupted traditional print media by empowering individuals to self-publish and share content without the need for traditional publishing houses.

4. **New Organizational Models and Revenue Streams**
   The internet has given rise to new organizational models based on big data, persuasive techniques, and innovative products and revenue models. It has brought a paradigm shift in doing business.

5. **Behavior Change and Cultural Shift**
   The internet has facilitated many forms of behavioral change and cultural shifts, leading to phenomena such as smartphone addiction and the emergence of actions like linking, liking, and swiping as significant tasks in daily life.

> ### Behavioral change
>
> One notable new behavior that emerged due to the rise of the internet is the sharing economy. The concept of sharing resources, services and goods on a large scale through online platforms was not widely imaginable before the internet became prevalent.
>
> For example, peer-to-peer platforms like Airbnb and Uber have transformed the way people utilize their assets. Airbnb allows individuals to rent out their homes or rooms to travelers, enabling a decentralized and more personalized alternative to traditional hotels. Uber provides a platform for people to offer ridesharing services using their vehicles, creating a new form of transportation service.
>
> These platforms leverage technology, online connectivity, and user trust systems to facilitate transactions and interactions between strangers. Before the internet, the idea of easily renting out a room in your house to a stranger or arranging a ride with someone you don't know through a mobile app was not a common or easily conceivable behavior.
>
> The internet's ability to connect people globally, coupled with advancements in digital payment systems and peer-to-peer communication, has led to the emergence and widespread adoption of these sharing economy platforms, fundamentally changing how people access and utilize services and assets. This new behavior was made possible by the internet's capacity to facilitate connections and transactions between individuals in a way that was previously unimaginable.

Blackboard lesson of how the Internet has created new economic models and behaviors.

Understanding the principles of the internet in combination with Lean principles is essential to grasp the profound impact of Blockchain technology. To fully appreciate the potential of blockchain and navigate its transformative effects, it's crucial to break free from traditional thinking and not be bound by the status quo or resistance to change.

This chapter draws a comparison between the principles of Lean and the principles of Blockchain technology, providing a framework for embracing this innovative technology and its potential.

The Seven Blockchain Principles

In this book, we often refer to the internet as Web 2.0 and Blockchain as Web 3.0. However, for Blockchain technology to function, it does require the internet as a communication layer. Blockchain is an evolution in how the internet is used rather than a complete stand-alone technology. Some of the principles of the internet do also apply to blockchain; however, blockchain has several of its own principles that are separate from internet principles.

We examine seven key principles of Blockchain technology, which are the basis of its power to transform business and society for the better.

1. Remove Intermediaries (See Figure 5.2)

Blockchain technology transforms the flow of value between the parties involved in a transaction by eliminating intermediaries. Intermediaries (sometimes referred to as "middlemen") are a common source of bottlenecks in traditional systems. Intermediaries have traditionally been considered to be "Essential Non Value Added" or "Type 1 Muda"[3]. This traditional dependence on intermediaries has resulted in slower transactions, higher costs, and exposure to centralized or single points of failure.

Blockchain's revolutionary impact lies in the decentralization of transactions through a distributed ledger. Unlike traditional centralized systems that rely on intermediaries such as brokers or third-party institutions, blockchain facilitates direct peer-to-peer transactions and removes the need for intermediaries. This direct interaction accelerates the value exchange between involved parties and reduces transactional friction.

This decentralization is achieved by using networks of computers (nodes), where data and applications are distributed across the network, eliminating dependence on a single controlling authority. This disintermediation eliminates the need for third-party "middlemen", significantly streamlining **trust in value flow** and making processes **more** predictable.

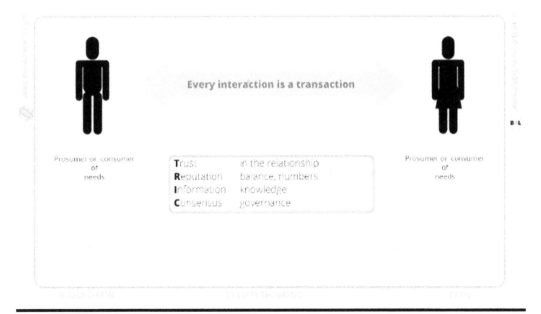

Figure 5.2   Removal of intermediaries between transactions significantly streamlines value flow and makes processes more predictable.

Business Rules and Standard Operating Procedures Automated

A crucial aspect that contributes to removing bottlenecks is the integration of smart contracts—a cornerstone of Blockchain technology. These self-executing contracts, embedded directly into the blockchain, automatically enforce and execute agreements when predefined conditions are met. Their automated and trustless nature eliminates the need for intermediaries, ensuring seamless and secure transactions.

Furthermore, blockchain's inherent transparency and immutability guarantee the secure recording of all transactions, making changes impossible. This feature adds an extra layer of trust without relying on intermediaries.

Essentially, blockchain's elimination of intermediaries and its decentralized, transparent, and secure framework play a crucial role in reducing barriers to the flow of value. This streamlined process promotes faster, more cost-effective, and more secure transactions, effectively eliminating traditional bottlenecks common in centralized systems.

It does not require a Kaizen approach to the existing process, but a radical change in the way we work. In Lean philosophy, it is called a **Lean Kakushin** event.

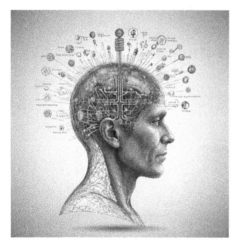

"In most organizations, the bottleneck is at the top of the bottle".
– Peter Drucker

2. Add Simplicity

Less is more: Simplicity promotes shared understanding and clarity.

Simplicity (inventive principle #2 in the TRIZ[4] methodology[5]: "Taking Out") is a guiding system design principle that Blockchain technology advocates for clarity and comprehension.

Blockchain's potential lies in simplifying and standardizing countless facets, ranging from product **identification** to individual and company identity proofs.

For example, unique product identification via barcodes and the ongoing efforts to establish a self-sovereign identity for individuals at a state, country, or region level are examples of this simplification.

Simplicity of standards underpins safety, quality, and consistency across our global landscape, driving efficiency across industries while protecting health and the environment. These international standards not only streamline processes and reduce waste but also promote compatibility, interoperability, and rapid product development.

Blockchain acts as a critical enabler for these standards, providing robust frameworks for governing entities, their interactions, regulation, governance, and resulting system designs. Compliance with these standards translates into reduced costs and time for manufacturers, improving collaboration, coordination, and communication in international trade. Ultimately, these standards build confidence among consumers and businesses, ensuring product reliability and enabling the selection of compatible offerings. It's working with "proofs" by design instead of (empty) promises which we have to control afterward.

Transparency, a crucial aspect guaranteed by blockchain, is achieved through its decentralized structure, immutability, and the automation of predefined business and interaction rules via **smart contracts**. These elements are in line with the principle that simplicity increases understanding and usability.

3. Prevention of Errors by Design

Blockchain technology is designed to preemptively stop errors and mistakes through a resilient, embedded mistake-proofing mechanism, similar to the Japanese principle of "Poka Yoke", but with the Poka Yoke seamlessly integrated into the system from the outset, ensuring error prevention by design.

The architecture includes several key features such as an immutable ledger, decentralized consensus, cryptographic security, smart contracts, traceability, error-checking mechanisms, auditing capabilities, and automated validation.

These elements work synergistically within the blockchain to prevent errors and increase accuracy through purposeful design.

Figure 5.3 shows examples of Poka Yoke (mistake proofing) for products, processes, and systems.

Figure 5.3   Product: Poka Yoke; Process: Poka Yoke; System: Poka Yoke.

Shared Source of Information

Blockchain disrupts the chaos caused by delayed information exchange, reducing errors and redundant data entry. It enables direct sharing from the source, promoting reliable dissemination of information. Furthermore, successful systems depend not only on enforcing compliance but also on encouraging active participation and motivation. Blockchain introduces a solution through token rewards, turning data sharing into a lucrative part of the business model.

Shared Purpose and Values

Tokens, as digital representations of assets or utilities on a blockchain, enable various functions such as value transfer, access to services, and active participation in decentralized ecosystems. By leveraging these design elements and encouraging collaborative data sharing through tokens, blockchain actively prevents errors and revolutionizes data management. This revolution improves data processing and promotes a landscape across all industries that is more secure, transparent, and efficient. In addition, there is clarity in advance about the purpose of the network, preventing many bureaucratic processes.

Capturing Value with Tokens and Cryptocurrencies

Web 3.0 introduces tokens: digital representations that enable various applications such as value transfer, access to services, and participation in decentralized ecosystems. These tokens and cryptocurrencies are integral components of blockchain, enhancing its functionality and promoting a seamless, value-driven digital environment.

4. Feedback

> "Your most unhappy customers are your greatest source of learning".
>
> **Bill Gates**

A well-known Lean visionary was named Taiichi Ohno[6]. He radically changed the production process at Toyota, Japan, in the 1970s and 1980s and was an architect of the Toyota Production System (TPS).

Ohno saw inefficiencies plaguing the factory floor—overproduction, inventory waste, waiting times, defects, and uneven workloads. Determined to bring change, he delved deep into the processes, seeking ways to improve and refine the system.

> "If you are going to do TPS you must do it all the way. You also need to change the way you think. You need to change how you look at things".
>
> – Taiichi Ohno

Ohno's philosophy echoed throughout the corridors of Toyota: Continuous improvement was imperative. He championed a culture where every employee's insight mattered. Their feedback was vital in identifying problems and spurring solutions. Ohno aimed not only to resolve immediate issues but to establish a culture of perpetual refinement—a pursuit for enhanced efficiency and quality ingrained in the company's DNA.

Fast forward to the digital age, where a different revolution is underway—one propelled by Blockchain technology. Like Ohno's quest to overhaul Toyota's manufacturing, blockchain introduces a new wave of tools for system enhancement, albeit in a digital age.

Blockchain, much like Ohno's approach, seeks to decentralize and streamline processes. It eliminates intermediaries, ushering in direct peer-to-peer transactions similar to Ohno's quest to remove bottlenecks in manufacturing workflows.

The innovation of smart contracts in blockchain mirrors Ohno's vision of standardized processes. These contracts automate agreements based on

LEAN BLOCKCHAIN KANBAN

Problem
Analysis
Solution

FOMO

Producer   Transporter   Wholesaler   Retailer   Consumer

Figure 5.4   Blockchain provides mechanisms for users to see system performance and status, from producer to customer through the full supply chain.

predefined conditions, much like Ohno's emphasis on standardized work procedures at Toyota.

Blockchain's transparency and immutability parallel Ohno's pursuit of traceability and error-proofing. Just as Ohno aimed to minimize defects and inconsistencies in manufacturing, blockchain's transparency reduces errors and ensures the integrity of digital transactions.

Moreover, **blockchain encourages a culture of feedback and continuous improvement**. It provides mechanisms for users to track and analyze system performance, from producer to customer, offering insights for ongoing refinements, problem-solving, analysis, and solutions. See Figure 5.4.

Lastly, akin to Ohno's promotion of collaboration and teamwork, blockchain's token economy incentivizes active participation. **It rewards users for contributing** or validating transactions, building on a collaborative ecosystem of innovation and improvement.

Network effects:
Blockchain technology is shifting from competition between companies to competition between networks.

In essence, while Taiichi Ohno's transformative efforts centered on optimizing manufacturing at Toyota, blockchain brings digital tools and approaches that transcend industries. Both share a common ethos—driving efficiency, reducing waste, and driving continuous improvement, each in their own unique domains and contexts.

What if there were a technology that could reward you for giving feedback or sharing information? What would that mean for our daily lives?

Many people are already addicted to their smartphones without receiving any compensation for it.

5. Consistency, Standardization, and Predefined Rules

Consistency is a cornerstone of effective processes, providing a stable framework that ensures predictability and reliability. It forms the bedrock of successful operations across various domains.

The Importance of Consistency

The concept of "doing 1% better every day" revolves around the idea of continuous improvement through consistent, incremental progress. It is based on the principle that making small, sustainable improvements every day can lead to significant growth and performance over time.

Consistency is the key to achieving long-term goals. By making small improvements every day, you will build momentum and develop a habit of progress. Even on days when you don't feel particularly motivated or inspired, focusing on just a 1% improvement every day for 365 days a year can lead to a 37.7 multiple increase over one year. See Figure 5.5.

When you're working toward a specific goal, the journey can sometimes feel overwhelming, especially if the goal is ambitious or long-term. Breaking it down into smaller, manageable tasks and focusing on improving a little each day will make the goal more achievable. Over time, these incremental improvements add up, bringing you closer to your ultimate goal.

Consistently making small improvements will maintain motivation and prevent burnout. Progress, no matter how small, gives a sense of satisfaction and strengthens the belief that you are making progress. This positive reinforcement can fuel your motivation to keep working toward your goals, even when you face challenges or setbacks.

Seeing tangible progress, no matter how small, increases self-confidence and self-esteem. As you consistently improve and achieve small victories, you will develop a stronger belief in your ability to overcome obstacles and

SMALL CHANGE, BIG IMPACT

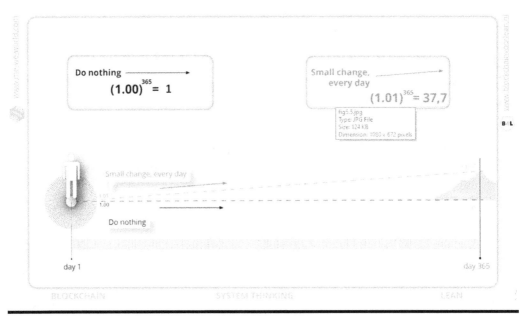

Figure 5.5 A 1% improvement every day for 365 days a yearcan lead to a 37.7 multiple increase over one year.

achieve your goals. This increased confidence further strengthens your commitment to continuous improvement.

Blockchain Enables Consistency

With Blockchain technology, procedures are consistent and standardized by its design. This prevents the likelihood of deviations that may lead to mistakes or inefficiencies. The system design promotes consistency, leading to smoother workflows, minimizing disruptions, and enhancing efficiency.

Moreover, maintaining consistency facilitates **better quality control**. By adhering to established procedures, organizations can consistently deliver products or services that meet **predefined quality standards**. This reliability not only instills trust in customers but also serves as a foundation for building loyalty.

Consistent processes also play a crucial role in training and onboarding new employees. Standardized procedures make it easier to impart training, as clear guidelines and practices can be consistently applied. This leads to a quicker and smoother transition for new hires into their roles.

Furthermore, consistency helps to improve effective **decision-making** by providing reliable data and a clear understanding of processes. When information and procedures remain consistent, it becomes easier to analyze trends, identify patterns, and make informed decisions based on reliable data.

Additionally, a commitment to consistency creates **a culture of continuous improvement**. By establishing a baseline through consistent processes, organizations can evaluate performance effectively, pinpoint areas for enhancement, and implement changes for ongoing refinement and optimization.

In essence, consistency and standardization act as the foundation for successful operations, promoting efficiency, reliability, quality, and a foundation for evolution and growth across various aspects of an organization.

6. Flexibility and Agility

Flexibility in agile processes involves creating adaptable systems that respond to changes without disruption or extensive rework. It emphasizes adjusting, iterating, and evolving in response to new information, customer feedback, or market shifts.

Software development methodologies like Scrum and Agile exemplify flexibility. Scrum's sprint-based approach enables teams to develop tasks within time-boxed iterations and adapt based on feedback, allowing reprioritization for subsequent sprints. Kanban visualizes task flow, limits work in progress, and supports dynamic adjustments based on shifting priorities or emergent tasks.

Overall, flexibility in agile processes empowers teams to embrace change, promptly address customer needs, and continually improve work methods, ensuring adaptability and resilience in a dynamic environment.

Blockchain technology enhances flexibility in system designs in the following ways:

- Blockchain's smart contracts automate processes based on predefined conditions. Their decentralized nature enables collaborative decision-making, increased accountability, and ensuring more alignment and agile responses.
- Immutable records ensure transparent and unalterable data, allowing traceability and learning from past iterations.

- Tokenization incentivizes agile collaboration. Because tokens represent ownership or rights, it encourages participants to contribute within the network. Network participants are often mentioned as stakeholders. They benefit from network growth, which creates "skin in the game" processes.
- With blockchain improvement proposals, every stakeholder is able to make a proposal for system improvement. The intention is to optimize the functioning of the whole instead of improving only the separate parts. Every ecosystem partner will be more successful if the system is more successful. It's a "we all benefit" or win-win-win approach.
- Additionally, interoperability facilitates seamless integration across diverse systems, empowering agile and adaptable system designs.

7. Traceability, Visibility, and Provenance

Effective process design thrives on transparency, visibility, and being able to trace the **origins (provenance) of data**, **information**, **and transactions**.

Traceability tracks a product or transaction's journey, ensuring quality, regulatory compliance, and trust.

Visibility provides insight into process stages, enabling efficient decision-making and building trust among stakeholders.

Blockchain's innovation elevates traceability and visibility by creating indisputable time-stamped transaction records, enabling secure data access without a single control point, and automating decisions via smart contracts. See Figure 5.6.

This technology not only guarantees transparency but also enhances trust and accountability throughout product life cycles.

To understand blockchain and its true potential, software and network designers, architects, and developers need to adopt an open, lateral thinking[7] mindset. They should be prepared to redesign processes from scratch, challenging existing norms and practices.

Systems Thinking Principles

Systems Thinking is a holistic approach to understanding complex systems, emphasizing the interconnectedness of parts and their interactions.

Here are the main principles behind Systems Thinking:

1. **Holism:**
   Systems Thinking views systems as wholes greater than the sum of their parts. It recognizes that the behavior of a system cannot be understood solely by examining its individual components, but rather by understanding how these components interact and influence each other.

2. **Interconnectedness:**
   Systems Thinking emphasizes the interconnectedness of elements within a system and their relationships. It recognizes that changes in one part of a system can have ripple effects throughout the entire system.

3. **Feedback Loops:**
   Feedback loops are fundamental to Systems Thinking. They are the mechanisms through which a system maintains stability or undergoes change. Feedback can be either reinforcing (positive) or balancing (negative), influencing the system's behavior over time.

4. **Emergence:**
   Systems Thinking acknowledges the phenomenon of emergence, where complex system behavior arises from the interactions of simpler components. Emergent properties are not always predictable from the characteristics of individual parts and may require understanding the system as a whole.

5. **Non-Linearity:**
   Systems Thinking recognizes that relationships within systems are often nonlinear, meaning that minor changes can lead to disproportionately large effects (positive or negative). This nonlinear behavior can result in unexpected outcomes and system behavior.

6. **Boundaries:**
   Systems Thinking defines boundaries to delineate the system from its environment. Understanding the boundaries of a system is crucial for defining what is included in the analysis and what is considered external factors.

7. **Multiple Perspectives:**
Systems Thinking encourages considering multiple viewpoints and stakeholders when analyzing a system. Recognizing diverse perspectives helps in understanding the complexity of the system and identifying potential conflicts or opportunities for collaboration.

8. **Continuous Learning:**
Systems Thinking is iterative and encourages continuous learning and adaptation. It acknowledges that understanding complex systems is an ongoing process, and new insights may lead to revisions in understanding and approaches to managing the system.

Summary

Lean principles focus on continuous improvement, streamlining processes, and maximizing customer value. It involves understanding customer needs deeply, aligning objectives with a shared purpose, fostering clear communication, and implementing decentralized governance for effective monitoring and relationship management.

Blockchain principles, when integrated with Lean, further enhance these ideals by offering decentralized governance, transparent transactions, and immutable records. They reinforce customer-centricity by ensuring trust, transparency, and security in interactions. Blockchain's decentralized structure enhances stakeholder analysis, aligns objectives with a shared purpose, fosters clear communication, facilitates monitoring, and strengthens relationship management through innovative mechanisms like Proof of Attendance and loyalty rewards.

Systems Thinking principles help us to understand complex systems, emphasizing the interconnectedness of parts and their interactions.

Systems Thinking recognizes that the behavior of a system can only be truly optimized by understanding how all components and inflows and outflows interact and influence each other. Together, Lean, Blockchain, and Systems Thinking principles create a framework that revolves around customer needs, transparent operations, and collaborative relationships, paving the way for sustainable success and continuous improvement within organizations.

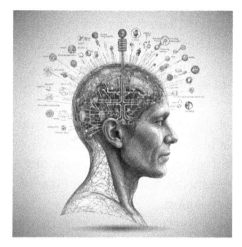

System Thinking involves empowering every element within a system, whether objects, businesses, individuals, or resources, by defining their roles and collectively establishing the system's objectives, rules, relationships, and resources. This approach leads to enhanced predictability, transparency, and clarity of outcomes.

Rather than offering a definitive solution, this process leads us to a transformed network status, as solutions themselves are not singular entities. Instead, it guides us toward a new configuration that embodies enhanced functionality and alignment within the network.

A Story of BlockchainLeanville

Once upon a time in the land of BlockchainLeanville, there existed a sprawling network of villages connected through a complex system of trade, knowledge exchange, and resource sharing. The villagers, each a unique element in this interconnected web, thrived on collaboration, coordination, and effective communication.

In the heart of BlockchainLeanville, a central square bustles with activity. This was where the villagers converged to discuss their system—their collective goals, the rules guiding their interactions, and the resources they shared. This dynamic system operated on the Lean Blockchain principles.

The village leaders, equipped with smart contracts coded into the very fabric of their communication network, facilitated decentralized decision-making. These contracts, transparent and immutable, built trust among villagers, assuring them that their transactions and agreements were secure and fair.

Motivation and engagement flourished through a token-based reward system. Villagers were incentivized not only with tokens but also with reputations and loyalty rewards. This empowered them to actively contribute to the community's growth and success. Their engagement was integral to the village's prosperity.

Adopting an end-to-end process approach, the villagers aligned their activities with their shared purpose and goals. They streamlined their interconnected processes, ensuring that each action contributed to the collective goal. This Lean approach prevented redundant efforts and enhanced overall efficiency.

But the villagers were not content with just the status quo. They believed in constant system improvement. Using blockchain improvement proposals, they submitted ideas and incentives for enhancements. The community collectively reviewed and implemented improvements, fostering a culture of transparency, accountability, and continuous evolution.

Their decisions were evidence-based, relying on data and proof gathered from the network. Relationships among villagers and the environment mattered greatly. They actively nurtured these relationships, knowing that strong ties led to a resilient and thriving community.

In BlockchainLeanville, the system thrived because of its people, united under a common purpose and empowered by Lean Blockchain principles. Through their unwavering coordination, collective engagement, and relentless pursuit of improvement, BlockchainLeanville became a beacon of interconnectedness and mutual prosperity for all its villagers.

In this new paradigm, the value placed on not-knowing surpassed the traditional emphasis on knowing or possessing all-encompassing knowledge. Consequently, there was no longer a need for a government, a CEO, or any single individual presumed to hold all knowledge.

Notes

1. Covey, S. R. (2012). *The Seven Habits of Highly Effective People*. New York: Rosetta Books LLC.
2. Emerson, H. (1919). Twelve Principles of Efficiency.
3. Womack, J. P. and Jones, D. T. (2003). *Lean Thinking: Banish Waste and Create Wealth in Your Corporation*. Free Press.
4. Altshuller, G. S. (1984). *Creativity as an Exact Science: The Theory of the Solution of Inventive Problems*. Translated by A. Gordon Williams.
5. BriefHistoryOf TRIZ.pdf (xtriz.com): https://www.xtriz.com/. BriefHistoryOfTRIZ.pdf.
6. Taiichi Ohno: https://en.wikipedia.org/wiki/Taiichi_Ohno.

7. Lateral thinking is a manner of solving problems using an indirect and creative approach via reasoning that is not immediately obvious. It involves ideas that may not be obtainable using only traditional step-by-step logic. De Bono, E. (1992). Serious Creativity: Using the Power of Lateral Thinking to Create New Ideas.

Chapter 6

Building Blocks

"Find problems where you think none exist".
– Shigeo Shingo[1]

Learning Objectives

Upon completing this chapter, you will be familiar with:

- The Lean Way
- The Lean House
- The Lean Blockchain House
- Three component architecture
- Foundations of the Lean Blockchain House
- Five pillars of the Lean Blockchain House
- A practical application of the Lean Blockchain House

The Lean Way

Many corporations have built their production systems using Lean principles and given these systems names such as "The Toyota Production System," "The Caterpillar Way," and "The Nissan Way". We will use the term "The

 DOI: 10.4324/9781003599715-6

Lean Way" as a general term for any system that has used Lean principles in its core building blocks and its fundamental business architecture.

The Lean House

The "Lean House", or "House of Lean", is a useful metaphor that helps us to visualize the fundamental principles and building blocks of "The Lean Way".

In this chapter, we will visit the Lean House; see Figure 6.1 to understand its architecture. We will then explore how the innovative use of Blockchain technology can be used to further strengthen the Lean House. We will be using the "Lean Blockchain Way" of thinking. We will propose an updated design of the house and call it the "Lean Blockchain House", Figure 6.2.

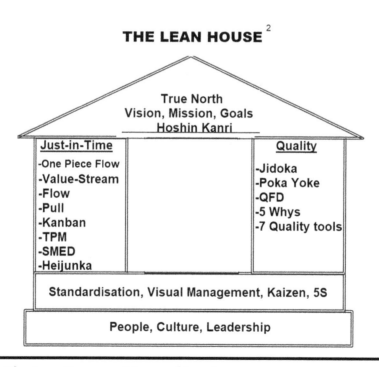

Figure 6.1 The Lean House or 'House of Lean'.

The Lean Blockchain House[3]

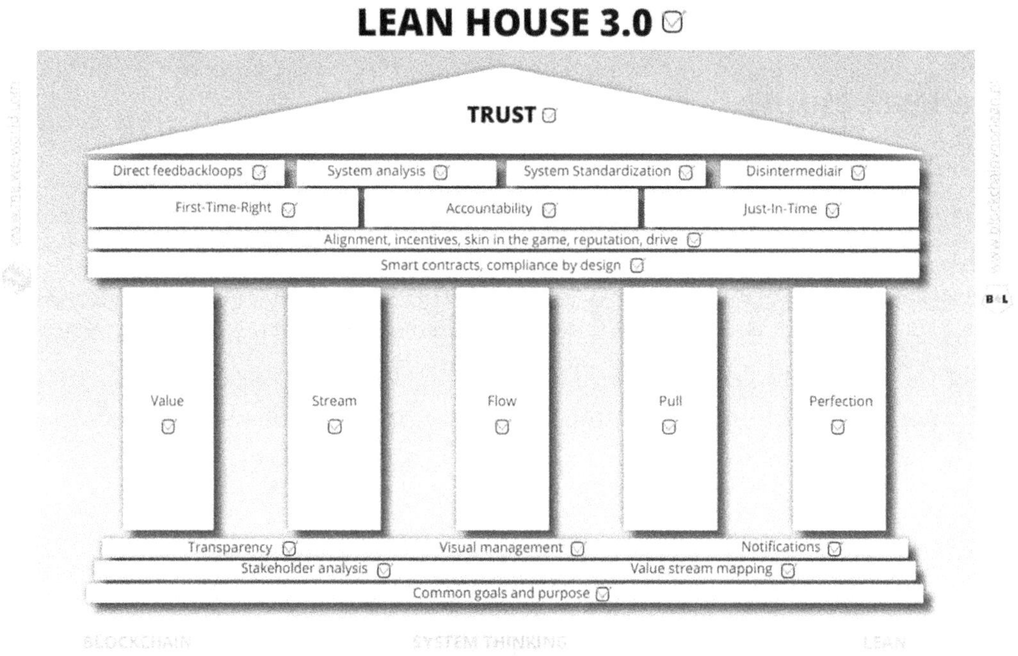

LEAN HOUSE 3.0 ☑

TRUST ☐

| Direct feedbackloops ☐ | System analysis ☐ | System Standardization ☐ | Disintermediair ☐ |
| First-Time-Right ☐ | Accountability ☐ | | Just-In-Time ☐ |

Alignment, incentives, skin in the game, reputation, drive ☐

Smart contracts, compliance by design ☐

B·L

| Value ☐ | Stream ☐ | Flow ☐ | Pull ☐ | Perfection ☐ |

Transparency ☐   Visual management ☐   Notifications ☐

Stakeholder analysis ☐   Value stream mapping ☐

Common goals and purpose ☐

BLOCKCHAIN   SYSTEM THINKING   LEAN

Figure 6.2   The Lean Blockchain House.

Three Component Architecture

The structures of both the Lean House and the Lean Blockchain House consist of three primary components:

1. Foundations: Core principles, the starting point from which the rest of the house is dependent. Without strong foundations, neither house can stand.
2. Pillars: The pillars of the Lean Blockchain House come from the original five core principles of Lean as proposed by Womack and Jones in 1996 [4].

3. Roof: The roof consists of elements that bind all of the other components together. It is what will protect the system from bad actors and individuals acting in their own selfish interests at the expense of the whole community (*vis-à-vis the tragedy of the commons[5]*)

We will now consider and explain each of these three components.

Foundations

The foundations of the Lean House have traditionally been conceptualized as being the culture, people, and leaders in the organization. It was fundamental to Toyota's success that they had full commitment and buy-in from all managers and employees. This is epitomized by the philosophy of the Honorary Chairman of Toyota Motor Corporation from 2006–2013, Fujio Cho[6], who said, "At Toyota we build people before we build cars".

Foundation of the Lean Blockchain House

The Lean Blockchain House chooses to have "Common Goals and Purpose" for its foundations. See Figure 6.3. This is because without common goals there can be no common direction and the house will not be "built straight". The house will collapse because each stakeholder and component in the system will be following their own ideas and goals. The foundation guides our motivations and provides a common and solid starting point for all the other components. This is epitomized by the famous quotation: "If a man knows not to which port he sails, no wind is favorable", by Lucius Annaeus Seneca the Younger (Seneca).[7]

Figure 6.3   Foundations of the Lean Blockchain House.

> **"If a man knows not to which port he sails, no wind is favorable"**
>
> Seneca
> 4 BC – AD 65

More About Common Goals and Purpose

Establishing and aligning common goals and purpose across the organization is essential for efficient and effective process design. It ensures everyone is working towards the same objectives, promoting unity, cooperation, and a shared sense of direction among team members. When goals are clearly defined and understood, it helps prioritize efforts and streamline activities.

The use of the internet for e-commerce is an example of a system where there is a huge disconnect between the goals of the various stakeholders in the system.

Take, for example, business package tracking using the internet. The customer can receive an update about the status of a package. Only one stakeholder provides this tracking service and therefore has therefore significant power and control. The information about the customer then becomes a product that they can sell. The customer becomes the product.

Is this aligned with the goals and values of the customer? Do the owners of the information care?

Consensus and Collaboration

The dynamics change when Blockchain technology is used in the system.

The consensus mechanisms built into the protocols of a blockchain prevent one stakeholder from making all decisions based on their goals alone.

A consensus is required by all stakeholders. Rules agreed upon by consensus can be "pre-coded" into a smart-contract[8] stored in a blockchain, and consensus protocols can also be used to ensure that rules have been obeyed for each transaction.

Blockchain technology becomes extremely useful when you need to collaborate on shared goals, purposes, and value(s).

Consensus is needed on the end value, the value-adding activities, the roles of stakeholders, and the objectives to be achieved. It requires Lean thinking, System Thinking, value thinking, and community consensus from the beginning to the end of the process.

Stakeholder Analysis

Understanding and analyzing stakeholders' interests, motivations, expectations, and influence within the organization is critical when forming the foundation.

This involves identifying all stakeholders (for example, employees, customers, suppliers, and shareholders) and understanding their needs and concerns.

This is also called understanding the "Voice of the Customer" (VOC), "Voice of the Business", and "Voice of the Network" (VON).

New Stakeholders to Consider

Concerns such as climate change, social inequality, and inclusivity are receiving increasing attention. We are witnessing a new wave of voices and needs, and new stakeholders who were overlooked in previous process designs.

Question?

Which model do you think will create more waste and externalities?

A. A competitive model or
B. A collaborative model

We must learn ways to transform from a competitive system design toward a more collaborative and inclusive ecosystem design.

Vertical Collaboration

Vertical collaboration occurs when stakeholders at different stages in the value stream collaborate. For example, a supplier collaborates with a customer.

The internet made the tracking and trace of business-to-consumer (B2C) packages possible. However, when the business has different motivations and goals from those of the customer, complexity arises, and collaboration is needed to find the optimal solution.

Horizontal Collaboration

Horizontal collaboration occurs within traditional organizations. For example, two different suppliers need to collaborate to complete one activity (the port services company unloading the containers and the shipping company holding the containers at the dock).

This complexity arises from various factors such as a lack of trust in collaboration, a competitive business model, and the loss of control over data.

In addition to the fact that companies find it difficult to collaborate on the basis of an internet-based infrastructure, the synchronization of ledgers and accounts balances is complex, time-consuming, and expensive. A shared system in which transfers of inflows and outflows of stock, information, or money are automatically updated would be the ideal final result (IFR).[9]

The Boston Consulting Group[10] has predicted that trade digitalization could increase revenues by 20%, cut processing time by 60%, and save global trade banks up to US $6 billion annually. The International Chamber of Commerce estimates paperless trade to create US $267 billion of additional exports among the G7 countries.

On July 20, 2023, the Law Commission's recommendations on electronic trade documents became law as the Electronic Trade Documents Act (ETDA) 2023 secured royal assent in the United Kingdom.

The UK Government has estimated that the Act will help to boost the UK's international trade—already worth more than £1.4 trillion—by providing benefits to UK businesses over the next 10 years of £1.1 billion.

The process of moving goods across borders involves a range of actors, including transportation, insurance, finance, and logistics service providers. The Commission estimates that global container shipping generates billions of paper documents a year. Across so many documents, the potential positive impacts of using electronic trade documents—including financial and efficiency gains, and environmental benefits—are vast.

Despite the size and sophistication of this market, many of its processes and the laws underlying them, are based on practices developed by merchants hundreds of years ago. In particular, under the current law of England and Wales, being the "holder" or having "possession" of a trade document has special significance. However, the law does not allow an electronic document to be possessed. As a result, nearly all documents used in international trade are still in paper form.

Over the past decade, the development of technologies such as distributed ledger technology has made trade based on electronic documents increasingly feasible. Without reform, the law would have lagged behind, hindering the adoption of electronic trade documents and preventing the significant associated benefits from being achieved.

Transparency

Transparency in Lean management involves open and clear communication across all levels of the organization. It ensures that information flows freely, enabling everyone to access relevant data and insights. Transparent practices improve trust in processes, encourage collaboration, and empower employees to make informed decisions, thereby enhancing overall efficiency.

Digitalization with Blockchain technology enables transparency for end-to-end processes and system designs.

Transparency could prevent questions about order status, input quality, provenance, location, authenticity, predictability of a process, etc.

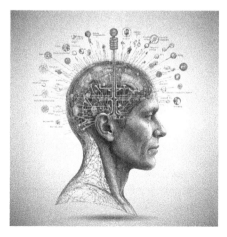

Understanding the difference between digitalization and digitization is important when discussing the use of Blockchain technology. **Digitization** denotes the process of converting analog data into digital format, exemplified by activities such as scanning physical documents or images. Conversely, **digitalization** involves the utilization of digital technologies to overhaul existing operational procedures, such as employing Blockchain technology or cloud services. Both digitization and digitalization play integral roles in facilitating a company's journey towards digital transformation.

Proof of Processing

Blockchain is sometimes called a *"network status technology"*. It enables different stakeholders to "fact-check" the status of the network with real-time updates, signals, or notifications. It streamlines the system functioning with quality proofs and trust in collaboration.

Question?

What do you think serves the insurance business model?

A. A transparent process design
B. A black box system design

The Five Pillars of the Lean Blockchain House

The pillars of the Lean Blockchain House come from the original five core principles of Lean as proposed by Womack and Jones in 1996. [11] See Figure 6.4.

Each of the five principles focuses on specific aspects crucial for Lean operations, reducing waste, and improving overall quality and efficiency.

2.1 Value

The concept of value is a central force that drives us to understand what customers really want and need in a product or service. It goes beyond mere transactional behavior.

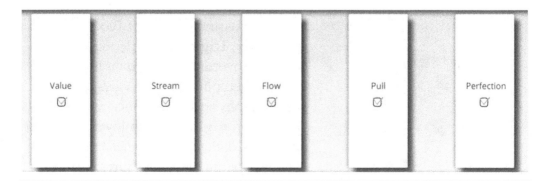

Figure 6.4   The Five Pillars of the Lean Blockchain House.

Prioritizing value directs efforts and resources toward activities that directly fulfill customer needs and eliminates those that contribute no value.

In today's landscape, the definition of value is expanding beyond traditional economic boundaries. In addition to ecological, social, and economic values, other facets are also gaining importance. Consider cultural, ethical, educational, health, and personal development values, in addition to innovation, technical, and political values. All these values together shape the world of human perspectives and priorities. To make it even more complex, different cultures and individuals may assign different degrees of importance to these values based on their unique perspectives and contexts.

Exchange of Value

The advent of Blockchain technology introduces a paradigm shift in the understanding and exchange of value. Cooperative technology is emerging, improving collaboration, inclusivity, and working towards shared goals. It outperforms competitive technology by promoting teamwork, innovation, and sustainability, prioritizing collective success over individual profit. This cooperative approach encourages open communication, knowledge sharing, and consideration of different perspectives, increasing overall efficiency and adaptability.

Blockchain technology is a part of the puzzle contributing to the global initiatives such as the Sustainable Development Goals (SDGs)[12]. See Figure 6.5. Collaborative technology harmonizes economic growth, social inclusion, and environmental protection for sustainable development in its design.

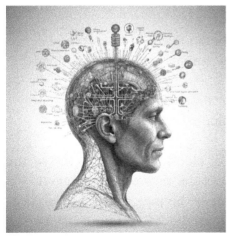

The SDGs, also known as the Global Goals, were adopted by the United Nations in 2015 as a universal call to action to end poverty, protect the planet, and ensure that by 2030 all people will enjoy peace and prosperity. To achieve sustainable development, it is crucial to harmonize three core elements: economic growth, social inclusion, and environmental protection. These elements are interconnected and are all crucial for the well-being of individuals and societies.

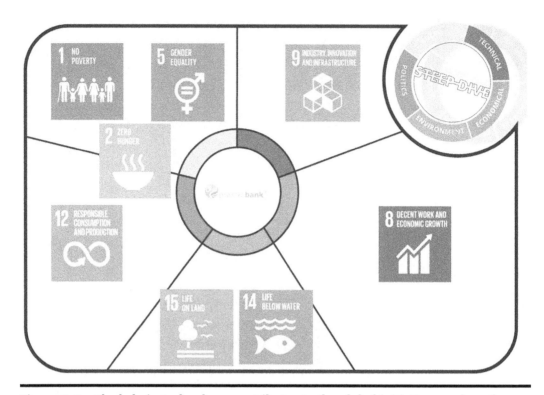

Figure 6.5 Blockchain technology contributes to the global initiatives such as the United Nations Sustainable Development Goals (SDGs) as used to reduce plastic waste in the ocean.

So, blockchain is an enabler to integrate and focus on value(s) that is no longer limited to just the economic domain. The technology introduces new possibilities to process multiple values in each transaction. You could define a transaction as an **interaction of value**. By recording the transaction, it gives the sender or receiver value in a social context.

The transparency of systems, smart collaboration rules, instant feedback loops, and immutable data are technical improvements that add value and accountability throughout the process. Other new features that blockchain introduces to manage value are tokenization (collective ownership and accountability) and the way in which value is captured, stored, and exchanged.

The decentralized and immutable nature of blockchain ensures the secure capture and storage of value. The joint effort of the network, distributed ledger, and cryptographic techniques guarantees the integrity and reliability of stored data. Consensus mechanisms, smart contracts, and permissioned or permissionless blockchains further strengthen security, transparency, and trust in the value exchange processes.

At its core, Blockchain technology brings new opportunities for cooperative and sustainable practices, providing a secure, transparent, and accountable framework for capturing, storing, and exchanging value. This transformative journey aligns economic activities with broader social and environmental goals, marking a profound shift toward a future where value is not just traded, but co-created, shared, and sustained.

If we look at trade finance, for example, Blockchain technology is able to digitize paper documents flow. It harmonizes the settlement and cooperation between all stakeholders that currently have to work with millions of paper documents per year. It includes financial gains by improved efficiency, but also social and environmental benefits.

2.2 *Value Stream*

Value stream refers to the end-to-end sequence of processes and actions involved in delivering a product or service to the customer. Value stream mapping helps visualize and analyze these processes, distinguishing between value-adding activities (those that directly contribute to meeting customer needs) and non-value-adding activities (waste).

Understanding the value stream enables organizations to optimize processes and eliminate inefficiencies.

2.3 *Flow*

Flow emphasizes the smooth and uninterrupted movement of work through the value stream. It involves minimizing interruptions, delays, or bottlenecks in the process to ensure a continuous and steady flow of work. By enhancing flow, organizations reduce lead times, improve responsiveness, and increase productivity.

2.4 *Pull*

Pull involves producing goods or services based on actual customer demand rather than speculative forecasts. Instead of pushing products into the market based on production schedules, the pull principle involves producing only what customers request or require. This strategy reduces excess inventory, minimizes waste, and ensures that resources are utilized efficiently.

2.5 **Perfection**

Perfection is an ongoing pursuit of continuous improvement and excellence in all aspects of operations. It involves striving for perfection in processes, products, and systems by continuously eliminating waste, improving efficiency, and innovating to meet changing customer needs. Perfection is a long-term goal that encourages a culture of continuous learning and improvement within an organization.

The Roof of the Lean Blockchain House

Despite having a solid foundation and robust pillars, the house would face significant challenges if it had a leaking roof! See Figure 6.6. The roof serves as the common shelter under which all the other components are protected. It binds the other components together.

What are the essential components for a roof?

A roof enables and facilitates trust in collaboration, the good of businesses, the good of people, and the good of society as a whole.

Smart Contracts, Trust by Design

In traditional processes, intentions are usually documented in agreements, general terms and conditions, or on websites. Unlike traditional process design, which controls and reviews events after the fact, Web 3.0 prioritizes immediate and transparent execution through data sharing, ownership, and established protocols.

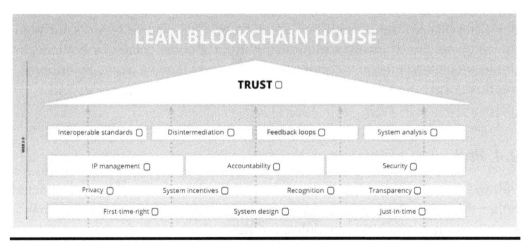

Figure 6.6   The roof of the Lean Blockchain House.

Example

In a traditional e-commerce environment, a buyer's intent to purchase a product is captured in the terms and conditions (Ts & Cs), and then the transaction details are confirmed after the purchase.

When things go wrong, that's when the trouble begins. Then you must try to correct things through correspondence, with an insurer or even through legal proceedings. It is a very unpredictable process, expensive, and frustrating for all parties.

In a Web 3.0 scenario, a smart contract on a blockchain can protocolize the buyer's intent and automatically execute the transaction once the conditions (such as payment confirmation or receiving a package) are met. This ensures immediate and transparent fulfillment of the buyer's intent, without the need for post-transaction checks.

Smart contracts, which are self-executing contracts with predefined rules, can automate various aspects. For instance, smart contracts could automatically trigger orders for raw materials when inventory levels drop to a certain threshold, aligning with just-in-time (JIT) principles.

By implementing smart contracts in a blockchain-based supply chain, organizations can create a more responsive, efficient, and collaborative ecosystem. The automation of processes (if this, then that), coupled with real-time data sharing and trust-building features, contributes to a reduction in the bullwhip effect and enhances overall supply chain resilience.

Alignment, Incentives, Skin in the Game, Reputation, and Drive

Blockchain's distributed and immutable ledger ensures transparency in transactions and promotes accountability through immutable data visible to network participants.

This improves process design by creating "skin in the game processes," seamlessly integrating ownership and responsibility.

Blockchain facilitates the formation of Decentralized Autonomous Organizations (DAOs). These are digital entities that are governed by smart contracts and community consensus mechanisms. This decentralization of decision-making allows participants to directly influence organizational decisions, creating a more responsive and involved network. Blockchain restructures the management layer of the organization by giving participants a voice, taking into account individual preferences, as well as the sustainable functioning of the whole.

The operational reward and incentive structure of a DAO is known as the "tokenomics" of a DAO. Tokenomics is part of the governance structure and addresses critical questions such as the total amount of token rewards distribution and inflation levels. It also serves as a valuable tool for identifying, aligning, and motivating participants.

Incentive Mechanisms

Tokens or cryptocurrencies can be used as incentives. The reward can be given in different ways:

- Participants can be rewarded with tokens for their contributions to the success of the network.
- A reward can follow from a price increase. If a network is successful, the demand for this token will increase, and if the demand is greater than the token supply, the price of the token will rise.
- Tokens can also be used to build a **reputation** within the network. Such a reputation is a reward in a social context, but it can also bring greater power.

In a token economy, reputation can become an important instrument to manage ownership, intellectual property, and contributions. It encourages individuals to act in ways that enhance rather than harm their reputation.

First-Time-Right

The essence of "first-time-right" or "right-first-time" is the concept of products and services that meet quality standards and customer expectations the first time they are received.

First-time-right requires the coherence and integrity of data throughout the production cycle. It is important that information quality is captured, shared, and can be tracked over the entire lifecycle of products and services without loss or corruption.

Blockchain serves as a catalyst for establishing **proofs of origin**, cross-border **track-and-trace** capabilities, and promoting a decentralized marketplace. In this environment, consumers prioritize products with verified origins and ethical practices. Companies that emphasize transparency, inclusivity, and sustainability gain a competitive advantage in this evolving and complex landscape.

Accountability

Accountability is the obligation to act on actions, decisions, and performance. It means taking responsibility for outcomes, both positive and negative, in personal, professional, or organizational contexts. This commitment involves transparency, integrity, and acceptance of the consequences of your behavior.

An example of the lack of accountability is the use of disposable plastic.

Consider the packaging sector. Many industries, including food and beverage, electronics, and consumer goods, rely heavily on plastic packaging due to its versatility, durability, and cost-effectiveness. While plastic packaging has several benefits, it also contributes significantly to the global plastic waste problem.

The lack of responsibility for plastic waste is clearly visible at different stages of the product life cycle. For example, manufacturers can prioritize cost-efficiency and convenience by using single-use plastic packaging, which is often discarded after a short period of use. End users, in turn, may improperly dispose of the packaging, leading to environmental pollution.

The challenge lies in the fact that responsibility for plastic waste management is often fragmented and lacks a comprehensive approach. Many industries and consumers do not have robust systems in place to collect, recycle, or properly dispose of plastic waste. In many cases, plastic waste ends up in landfills, water bodies, or incineration, causing harm to ecosystems and wildlife.[13]

Governments, industries, and consumers all have a role to play in tackling this problem. The lack of a uniform and responsible approach to plastic waste management contributes to the perpetuation of the environmental problems associated with plastic pollution. Initiatives such as extended producer responsibility and increased awareness of sustainable practices are crucial steps toward improving responsibility for plastic waste throughout its life cycle.

Profit, People, and Planet[14]

In 1994, John Elkington coined the phrase "Triple Bottom Line" of People, Planet, and Profit (also known as the 3Ps).

The idea behind the "3Ps" is that in order for companies to measure their true value, they should use three separate performance indicators. These should focus on profit but also the organization's social (people) and environmental (planet) impact.

Taking responsibility for the outcomes of all stakeholders: business owners/shareholders (profit), social (people), and the environment (planet).[55]

Blockchain protocols can be used to establish an open standard for creating verifiable claims about changes in the state of the world. These claims serve as the basis for creating unique digital assets, such as non-fungible tokens, representing real-world identities, relations, and outcomes.

By leveraging decentralized web standards, blockchain networks can implement advanced features like linked data, decentralized identifiers, and verifiable credentials. This ensures a high level of security and transparency in the creation and management of digital assets.

Applications built on this new digital infrastructure have the potential to revolutionize how sustainable impact is financed, measured, valued, and traded. This includes various forms of capital flowing into social, environmental, and economic development.

Furthermore, community currencies within this system can drive outcomes toward local social and economic development goals in inclusive, locally governed, low-risk, and sustainable ways. The innovation potential includes new economic models, incentive schemes, investment mechanisms, and community sustainability approaches.

Just-in-Time

Just-in-time in production and inventory management was first used by the Toyota Motor Company[15] and now typically refers to a strategy where materials and products are delivered or produced precisely when they are needed, minimizing inventory costs and maximizing efficiency. The word "just" in this context means "precisely" or "exactly", indicating the importance of timing.

However, if we consider the word "just" to mean "fair", as it does in the context of "justice", the phrase could be interpreted in a different light. Here's how:

1. "Fair" as in Equitable or Adequate:
   - When "just" is translated to "fair", it implies something that is equitable, proper, or adequate. "Fair" timing would mean the timing is appropriate and balanced, neither too early nor too late.
2. Reinterpretation of "Just-in-Time":
   - If "just" means "fair", then "JIT" could be understood as "fair in time" or "in a fair amount of time". This interpretation would shift the

focus from precision to appropriateness. It implies that the timing is reasonable and sufficient for the needs at hand, allowing processes to flow smoothly without unnecessary rush or delay.

3. Conceptual Alignment:
   – In both interpretations, the underlying principle is about optimization. The traditional "JIT" focuses on precision to reduce waste and increase efficiency. The "Fair in time" interpretation would focus on fairness in timing, ensuring that resources are provided in a manner that is balanced and just, aligning with the broader goals of fairness and adequacy in operations.

Is it better to be informed that there is a need for more milk precisely at the point when there is no milk remaining in the bottle? Or is it better to be informed in a "fair amount of time" before the level of milk gets too low? See Figure 6.7.

Figure 6.7   Kanban for buying more milk. The kanban signal is the level of the milk.

The JIT operates on a **pull system**, where the initiation of production is triggered by customer demand. Instead of pushing products into the market, the system responds to actual orders or consumption.

Quality Control and Traceability

Blockchain's ability to record every step in the production process can be leveraged to ensure quality control and traceability of products. Defects, recalls, and deviations can be traced back to their origins, allowing for quicker identification of issues and more targeted solutions. This aligns with the Lean principle of Jidoka (autonomation), where processes are designed to detect abnormalities.

"Where there is no standard, there can be no improvement. For these reasons, standards are the basis for both maintenance and improvement".
– Masaaki Imai[16]

System Standards

Blockchain goes beyond digitization to digitalization, encouraging collaboration in end-to-end processes and making it possible to integrate international standards. Complying with international standards leads to increased efficiency and reduced carbon emissions. There are already standards, but the problem is there is no confidence in the data and less accountability included in the process design. It's mostly words or promises, with little action.

Working with standards ensures accountability and responsibility and makes alignment with the SDGs possible. Besides that, blockchain could bring transparency in every interaction following predefined collaboration rules. With direct feedback loops and improvement proposals, a culture of more and more value creation can be achieved.

System Analysis

A lack of coordinated collaboration has led to fragmented data, conflicting interests, unethical behavior, centralized power, and a lot of non-value-added work, creating waste by design. Complexity arises from different standards between organizations, sectors, and countries, coupled with unclear legislation. Within organizations, the absence of standardized policies, processes, functions, roles, and systems increases the challenge, creating a highly complex collaborative environment.

Lean thinking underlines the importance of continuous improvement. But what if the **fundamental elements are flawed**? Improvements might then focus on the symptoms, failing to address the root cause and resulting in suboptimal outcomes. Should we call this Lean washing?

An example:

In a multinational corporation, departments operate with different data management practices, creating confusion and hindering cross-functional collaboration. Conflicting interests among teams lead to inefficiencies, and unethical actions go unchecked due to a lack of standardized ethical guidelines. This lack of cohesion results in a concentration of power at the executive level, leaving lower-level employees feeling disempowered.

The complexity deepens as the corporation operates in various countries, each with its own set of regulations, board members, shareholders, and compliance requirements. Additionally, within the organization, different departments follow disparate processes and lack standardized roles and systems, making it challenging to achieve seamless collaboration.

Applying Lean thinking, the company decided to implement continuous improvement initiatives. However, the improvements made in individual departments addressed only surface-level issues, such as workflow inefficiencies, without tackling the fundamental problems of inconsistent standards and power imbalances. As a result, despite efforts to enhance efficiency, the organization continued to face suboptimal outcomes due to the persistent lack of harmonized collaboration and foundational flaws.

A fundamental change in the entire operational framework is essential. This requires a transformative process, commonly called a **paradigm shift**. Without an efficient collaborative model, we find ourselves entangled in the unnecessary circulation of waste. It is critical to recognize that our organizational model inherently generates waste.

If we do not improve the system and solely focus on reducing waste in a system context, then we have learned nothing from all the archetypes described by great systems thinkers such as Donella Meadows, Jay W. Forrester, Peter Senge, and Russell L. Ackoff.

** We won't delve deeper into archetypes, a topic we recommend for further exploration. This chapter serves solely as an introduction to Lean System Thinking and its building blocks.

Trust

Reflecting on the evolution of trust and its foundations, we could outline the following progression:

1. Trust in God,
2. Trust in communities,
3. Trust in government,
4. Trust in code.

This progression broadly summarizes the historical shift in the foundations of trust between people. It started with trust in faith, followed by trust in local communities (with or without a king or leader), and then in institutions. Finally, we now trust in the reliability and integrity of code. All these mechanisms bring people together to collaborate, coordinate, and communicate.

The effectiveness of collaboration is crucial in Lean manufacturing. The availability of information is often an important part of working effectively. We can also deduce this from our traditional black box organizational designs. **Because we have no insight into the inflows and outflows of the entire chain, we have to make predictive forecasts.**

Therefore, if we don't want to say no to the customer, we always produce or order more stock than the market needs.

With blockchain, we have access to technology that integrates trust into its process design. The key elements that make this possible are cryptographic principles, decentralization, transparency, predefined consensus mechanisms, and direct feedback loops.

Disintermediation

This is a transformation from the traditional reliance on centralized authorities for trust in internet-based infrastructure. Blockchain's trust in code promotes a more secure, transparent, and resilient system for various applications, including financial transactions and supply chain management.

While blockchain holds significant promise, its implementation requires careful consideration of technical, regulatory, and organizational challenges.

The Lean House framework requires a strategic approach that aligns with the organization's goals and purpose of end-to-end processes.

Key Benefits and Blockchain Enablers

- Decentralized trust, cryptography
- Quality by design, smart contracts, and timestamps
- System goals, Voice of the Network (VoN)
- Enhanced transparency, permissionless ledger
- Improved traceability, transparency
- Efficient coordination, standards
- Automated processes, standard operating procedures automated
- Real-time data insights, 24/7 available
- Secure data sharing, zero knowledge proofs
- Reduced fraud and errors, control by design
- Continuous system improvement, blockchain improvement proposals
- Environmental sustainability, no central authority, or single point of failure

Advantage of the Lean Blockchain Way

Common Goals and Purpose

Adopting a Lean blockchain way of working has the potential to revolutionize traditional processes by combining the principles of Lean manufacturing with the transparency, efficiency, and security of Blockchain technology. It can lead to more streamlined, accountable, and collaborative operations that are aligned with both Lean philosophies and the demands of the modern digital age.

Example: Supply chain management

Let's consider a company that specializes in organic food products. Traditionally, the supply chain for these products involves multiple parties—farmers, distributors, processors, and retailers. With the use of Blockchain technology, this supply chain can be reimagined and redesigned to bring significantly more value in the following areas:

Transparency and Traceability

Implementing a blockchain-based system allows every step of the supply chain to be recorded as immutable transactions on a shared ledger. Each organic product can be tagged with a unique identifier (like a QR code) linked to its transaction history on the blockchain.

Consumers can scan the code and trace the journey of the product from farm to table, verifying its authenticity and organic certification.

Enhanced Trust and Quality Assurance

With transparent and immutable records, consumers can have increased trust in the authenticity of organic claims. Farmers can record crucial data such as planting, harvesting, and processing methods, which cannot be altered or tampered with. This builds confidence in the quality and ethical standards of the product.

Efficiency and Reduced Fraud

Smart contracts, programmable self-executing contracts on the blockchain, can automate various processes. For instance, payments can be automatically triggered when predefined conditions (like successful delivery or quality checks) are met, reducing delays and the risk of fraudulent activities in payments or supply chain disruptions.

Alignment

Fractionalized ownership allows various stakeholders, including consumers or investors, to own a portion of high-value assets, such as farmland or processing facilities, represented as tokens on the blockchain. This democratizes investment opportunities, enabling individuals to participate in ownership who may not afford an entire asset.

For instance, consumers who value supporting ethical farming practices and the organic food industry can invest in fractional ownership of farmland through tokens. This creates a sense of ownership and alignment with the values of the organization, building a stronger consumer-business relationship.

Incentives

Token-based reward systems can incentivize stakeholders to participate actively in the supply chain. For instance, farmers could earn tokens for implementing sustainable practices or meeting specific quality standards. These tokens represent a share of the value created or saved due to their contributions.

Consumers scanning QR codes or engaging in eco-friendly behaviors (like recycling packaging) could receive tokens as rewards. These tokens can be redeemed for discounts on organic products or other benefits, encouraging more engagement and loyalty.

Tokenized incentives create a relationship between stakeholders by rewarding behaviors that align with the goals of the system.

Overall, by implementing fractionalized ownership and token reward incentives on the blockchain in this supply chain scenario, stakeholders are not just passive participants but become active contributors, creating a shared ecosystem where value creation is rewarded and distributed more equitably among the participants. This helps reinforce transparency, trust, and sustainability while fostering a more engaged and loyal community around the organic food supply chain.

By reimagining the value within the supply chain through Blockchain technology, this example showcases how transparency, trust, efficiency, and sustainability can be significantly enhanced, creating new forms of value for both businesses and consumers.

Reputation

In addition, blockchain can enable the tracking of fair-trade practices and sustainable sourcing. It can certify fair compensation for farmers, track carbon footprint reductions, and incentivize eco-friendly practices. Consumers who value sustainability can make informed choices based on verified data stored on the blockchain.

Notes

1. Shingo, S. (1987). *The Sayings of Shigeo Shingo: Key Strategies for Plant Improvement.* Page 18.
2. Lean House: This design is an interpretation by John Dennis (2024) based on many other proposed versions such as Jeffery Liker: The Toyota Way (2004).
3. Tesser, M. (2020). *The Lean Blockchain House.*
4. The 5 Principles of Lean as explained in the book *The Machine That Changed the World* Womack and Jones (1996).
5. Hardin, G. The Idea of the Tragedy of the Commons Was Made Popular by the American Ecologist. https://www.garretthardinsociety.org/articles/art_tragedy_of_the_commons.html.

6. Fujio Cho, Honorary Chairman of Toyota Motor Corporation, https://en.wikipedia.org/wiki/Fujio_Cho.
7. Wikipedia. Seneca the Younge. https://en.wikipedia.org/wiki/Seneca_the_Younger.
8. A smart contract is a computer program or a transaction protocol that is intended to automatically execute, control, or document events and actions according to the terms of a contract or an agreement: en.wikipedia.org/wiki/Smart_contract.
9. The ideal final result (IFR) was proposed by Henrich Altshuler in his TRIZ methodology (1946). IFR is the ultimate solution to a problem when the desired result is achieved by itself.
10. Flow report Deutsche bank: A guide to digital trade finance, published January 2024.
11. The 5 Principles of Lean as explained in the book *The Machine That Changed the World* Womack and Jones (1996).
12. THE 17 GOALS. Sustainable Development. https://sdgs.un.org/goals.
13. Rochman, C. M., et al., (2013). Policy Options for Plastic Waste in the Ocean. *Environmental Science & Technology*, 47(10), 3416–3427.
14. What the 3Ps of the Triple Bottom Line Really Mean. https://www.forbes.com/sites/jeroenkraaijenbrink/2019/12/10/what-the-3ps-of-the-triple-bottom-line-really-mean/.
15. Ohno, T. (1988). *Toyota Production System: Beyond Large-Scale Production.* Productivity Press.
16. Imai, M. (2012). *Gemba Kaizen: A Commonsense Approach to a Continuous Improvement Strategy*, Second Edition. McGraw Hill Professional.

Chapter 7

Procedures

In this chapter, we explore the concept of procedures and learn why we need standard operating procedures (SOPs). We delve into the definition of a procedure and trace their evolution in the context of the internet and cryptography.

Learning Objectives

Upon completing this chapter on procedures, you will be able to:

- Explain the importance of standard procedures
- Understand how procedures organize trust and the truth
- Comprehend the concepts of smart contracts
- Give some examples of cryptographic procedures
- Introduce "the oracle problem"

In this chapter, we look at the operation of procedures both in general and specifically in the procedures carried out by the intermediaries. In many cases, these procedures can be automated with "smart contracts". These are simple "if/when this happens then that is the outcome" (IFTTT).

A standard procedure is a procedure that one group of people has agreed that this is the right way to work. The agreements are recorded in a document where the specifications are described. If everyone agrees with this method, this method forms the standard.

DOI: 10.4324/9781003599715-7

"Coming together is a beginning. Keeping together is progress. Working together is success". Henry Ford

Why Do We Need Standard Procedures?

An SOP precisely outlines the method of performing work, encompassing details such as computer settings or configurations for various IT devices and machinery. It extends to specifying conditions, including ISO standards, for conducting control activities and verification audits. Understanding the concepts of a standard and a procedure sets the stage for appreciating how **consensus, trust, and truth** are structured.

> A procedure is the description of a series of actions and agreements to coordinate routine cross-functional (between departments of organizations) activities.
>
> In Chapter 9, we will talk about **standardization.** This is something different from standard procedures. When we talk about standardization, we mean a standard for products, materials, and services; the agreed specifications; the taxonomy.

Standard procedures play a crucial role in Lean management. Here's how standard procedures are integrated into Lean management:

What Is a Process?

A process is made up of a group of related procedures that together have a common goal.

Standardization of Processes

Lean management emphasizes the standardization of processes to reduce variability and enhance efficiency. Procedures serve as documented guidelines for standardizing tasks and activities, ensuring that everyone follows a consistent and optimized approach.

Continuous Improvement (Kaizen)

Lean management promotes a culture of continuous improvement, known as Kaizen. Standard procedures act as a baseline for improvement initiatives. Teams can identify inefficiencies or bottlenecks in existing procedures and work collaboratively to enhance and optimize them.

Waste Reduction

One of the primary goals of Lean management is the elimination of waste in all forms, such as overproduction, excess inventory, waiting times, and defects. Standard procedures help identify and address areas of waste by providing a clear framework for evaluating processes and identifying non-value-added activities.

Visual Management

Lean management often utilizes visual tools, such as kanban boards and visual cues, to enhance communication and understanding. Procedures can be represented visually to provide quick reference points, aiding in the easy understanding and adherence to standardized processes.

Employee Empowerment

Standard procedures serve as a tool for training and empowering employees, providing clear guidelines on how to perform tasks and contribute to process improvement.

Customer Focus

Standard procedures help ensure that processes are aligned with customer requirements, and any deviations are promptly addressed to enhance customer satisfaction.

Streamlining and Efficiency

Lean management seeks to streamline processes to improve overall efficiency. Standard procedures provide a structured framework for teams to identify and eliminate unnecessary steps, reducing complexity and improving the flow of work.

Data-Driven Decision-Making

Standard procedures can include guidelines for data collection and analysis, facilitating informed decision-making to drive continuous improvement.

In essence, standard procedures are an integral component of Lean management, serving as the foundation for continuous improvement, waste reduction, and the overall optimization of processes to deliver value to customers.

A Paradigm Shift in Trust, Truth, and Execution

Traditionally, organizations heavily rely on standard procedures, yet these optimizations often cater to individual goals rather than the holistic system. They tend to focus on "parts" rather than the entire end-to-end process.

Blockchain technology revolutionizes collaboration by embedding automated procedures into operational frameworks. See Figure 7.1.

PROCEDURES AUTOMATED

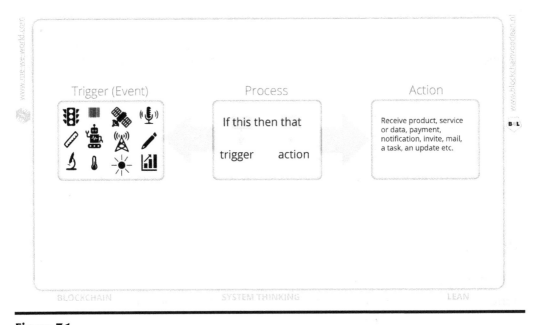

Figure 7.1

This paradigm shift involves agreements transforming into protocols, replacing third-party mediated trust and execution with cryptographic trust and automated procedures known as smart contracts.

Within a Lean framework, an integrated infrastructure incorporating Lean tools enhances overall process efficiency. Adopting a supermarket-model organization aligns the system's intentions with all stakeholders collaboratively.

"Anticipating and agreeing upon responsible parties and their intentions marks a pivotal shift".

This approach cultivates collective motivation for system-wide improvements, moving beyond isolated enhancements in specific components.

The shift is from human and paper-based trust and truth towards algorithmic and cryptographic trust and truth.

How Do We Organize Trust?

Throughout history, trust has traditionally been anchored in third parties and paper promises, shaping the fabric of societal functions for decades. Intermediaries like banks, institutions, notaries, and the government have been integral to our accustomed way of operating.

When accomplishments need verification, these entities furnish copies that serve as evidence in social interactions. For instance, displaying a driver's license as proof of the right to drive a car has become a standard procedure.

This conventional SOP has become ingrained, and people seldom question if it is a Lean practice. There is a willingness to pay for these services when necessary, and until recently, there has not been a viable alternative.

Process in Code

The first use case or example that showed that things can be done differently was the birth of Bitcoin in 2009. Since then, there have been many iterations on this protocol to make this method more efficient and advanced. Today, this method is becoming more and more a reality and a new method for organizing processes based on code, for various use cases/industries.

Just as the first airplane could not carry the considerable number of passengers we carry in aviation today, the Bitcoin protocol of 2009 is also an early design of the full potential of cryptographic trust and truth. The concept demonstrates the ability to guarantee outcomes based on mathematical cryptographic calculations. The outcomes are the result of an automated standard procedure and community consensus.

What makes a process in code more Lean?

"Efficiency in a coded process embodies Lean principles by minimizing reliance on third-party dependencies. Collaborating with external entities often involves variables like their workforce, reliability, precision, availability, surplus inventory, consultancy expenses, workflow pace, logistics, inefficiencies, and errors.

Imagine holding absolute control over functions typically outsourced to a third-party. Being able to demonstrate real-time status updates to anyone, anywhere, at any moment signifies achieving a state of self-sovereignty".

Trust the Process

Blockchains serve as essential timestamping tools, capturing precise details—what occurred, where, and when—in specific events. The protocol stored in the blockchain, known as a smart contract, manages the balance of **storage inflow and outflow**.

Smart contracts function as automated executors of agreements, resembling digital contracts that autonomously execute terms based on predefined conditions. For instance, upon meeting conditions like receiving payment, a smart contract seamlessly progresses to the next step, transferring ownership of a digital asset.

This automated process, devoid of paperwork, emails, and third-party intervention, eradicates numerous inefficiencies inherent in traditional administration work. It alleviates tasks such as information retrieval, validation, printing, transportation, waiting times, and document completion.

Can you imagine that the transactional flow of your work will look more like a vending machine?

So you pick a product or service (recognized as a digital twin), pay the money (in crypto), and the vending machine registers (in the ledger) the shift in balances (debit and credit).

What Is the Truth?

The truth, traditionally reliant on paper-based processes, resides with intermediaries and legal channels. This long-standing organizational method involves significant manual work.

As highlighted, the blockchain paradigm eliminates the need for a "trusted third-party". Leveraging smart contracts in combination with standardized tokens enable consensus on the "truth" within the ecosystem and promotes the seamless interoperability of value streams.

Example of Cryptographic Trust

Let's consider a few simple examples where traditional paper-based or email-based processes can be transformed into blockchain smart contracts:

Real Estate Transactions

In traditional real estate dealings, multiple paper documents, legal agreements, and intermediaries such as notaries and title companies are involved. However, the use of smart contracts on a blockchain streamlines the transfer of ownership. Once payment is received, the smart contract autonomously updates ownership records and transfers the property title to the buyer, eliminating intermediaries.

Consider the appraisal process: Every transaction detail—parties involved, actions taken, location, and timing—related to real estate can be securely recorded on a blockchain. This comprehensive record forms an appraisal report and a complete history, acting as a "material or product passport" for a house without necessitating an appraiser.

Supply Chain Management

Supply chain management often relies on manual documentation for tracking products from manufacturing to delivery, leading to potential errors and delays. Smart contracts can be used to create a transparent and traceable supply chain. Each step in the process, from production to delivery, can be recorded on the blockchain, ensuring accuracy and efficiency.

Insurance Claims Processing

Insurance claims typically involve extensive paperwork, verification processes, and manual reviews, leading to delays in claim settlements. Smart contracts can automate the claims process. When predefined conditions (such as the occurrence of a covered event) are met, the contract can automatically trigger the disbursement of funds to the policyholder.

Digital Identity Verification

Identity verification often requires physical documents and manual checks, leading to security and privacy concerns. Smart contracts can be used for digital identity verification. Once an individual's identity is confirmed through secure means, a smart contract can generate a verifiable digital identity on the blockchain, enhancing security and privacy.

In November 2023, the European Digital Identity Wallet was officially finalized and embraced. Consider this digital wallet as your enchanted key to crucial documents—your ID, diplomas, or insurance policies—tucked away neatly in a mobile app that you have complete control over. Imagine effortlessly opening a bank account, establishing or proving a business, switching energy providers, accessing government services, or renting a car anywhere in Europe, all with the simplicity of using your digital wallet. Now that the decision has been made, it is expected that this way of working will become a reality by 2027.

Tokenized Real World Assets

Ownership of certain assets, like stocks or certificates, involves physical paperwork and reliance on centralized authorities for transfer. By tokenizing assets on a blockchain, ownership can be represented digitally through tokens. Smart contracts can facilitate the automatic transfer of these tokenized assets between parties when payment or conditions are met.

In each of these examples, the transition to blockchain smart contracts streamlines procedures and processes, reduces the need for intermediaries,

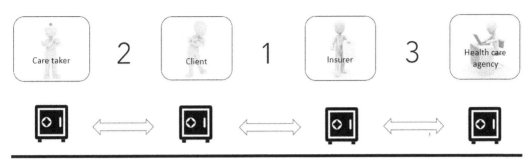

Figure 7.2   A healthcare transactional process example.

enhances transparency, and automates the execution of agreements based on predefined conditions.

Let's have a look at a simple blockchain-enabled healthcare use case following procedures with smart contract implementation and tokenization:

1. How Does This Work?

See Figure 7.2 for a typical healthcare transactional process.

☐ Tokenized representation: Step 1

The client's digital wallet contains tokens representing their allocated hours of care from the insurer, acting as verifiable proof of entitlement to healthcare services.

☐ Automated verification: Step 2

When the care is provided, the caretaker updates the service completion status within the blockchain network.

☐ Automatic payment: Step 3

Smart contracts trigger automatic payments from the insurer to the healthcare agency directly from the client's wallet, synchronizing token balances immediately with the provided care hours.

2. Benefits

■ Client empowerment: Clients have control via their digital wallets, improving convenience and trust in the healthcare process.

- Enhanced efficiency: Reduction in errors, audits, and bureaucracy due to automated processes, minimizing redundant data entry across multiple systems.
- Digital transformation: Completes the digitization of records and robust data management, improving information accuracy and accessibility.
- Streamlined collaboration: Improved collaboration among stakeholders, enabling more meaningful work and fostering ecosystem development.

3. Improvements

Synchronization of information, products/services and payments. See Figure 7.3.

- Elimination of waste: Removing unnecessary printing, transportation, and stocking of physical timesheets, reducing overproduction and redundant information entry
- Faster payments: Elimination of the 80-day waiting period, leading to quicker settlements and increased utilization of talent
- Reduced errors: Minimization of errors related to manual data handling, retyping, and transportation, enhancing accuracy and reliability
- Increased flexibility: Efficient data sharing in groups facilitates collaboration and adaptability in a rapidly changing healthcare landscape

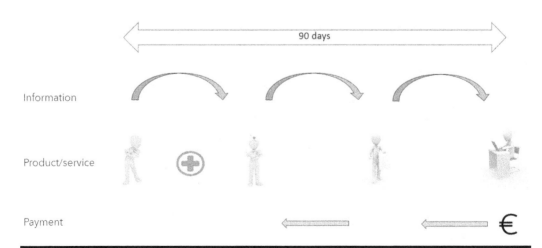

Figure 7.3 Synchronization of information, products/services and payments using a blockchain.

4. *Additional Considerations*

- Data security and privacy: Implement robust security measures to safeguard sensitive healthcare information within the blockchain network
- Regulatory compliance: Ensure adherence to healthcare regulations and compliance standards within the blockchain framework
- User education and adoption: Educate stakeholders on using the digital wallet and blockchain-based systems to maximize their benefits

Procedures Meets the Internet of Things

Decentralized Autonomous Agents

This syllabus primarily focuses on exploring the correlation between Lean and Blockchain. However, amid this exploration, the rapid disruption caused by artificial intelligence (AI) in operational procedures is evident. Therefore, we conclude with a definition of autonomous agents and some relevant quotations, recognizing the rapid progress taking place in this space.

What Are Autonomous Agents?

Autonomous agents are programs, powered by AI, that, when given an objective, can create tasks for themselves, complete tasks, create new tasks, reprioritize their task list, complete the new top task, and loop until their objective is reached. These agents never get tired, never quit their jobs, and don't complain about long working hours.

> "[Intelligent] autonomous agents are the natural endpoint of automation in general. In principle, an agent could be used to automate **any other process**.
> Once these agents become highly sophisticated and reliable, it is easy to imagine an exponential growth in automation across fields and industries".—Bojan Tunguz, Machine Learning at NVIDIA

> "Autonomous Agents are the next wave—not just in tech, but in business at large. I predict that within 10 years, there will be multiple billion-dollar companies run entirely by autonomous agents. It is inevitable".
> Ben Parr, Co-founder and president at Octane AI

Summary

Standard procedures are integral to daily life, offering essential structure, consistency, and guidance across diverse activities for reaching our goals. They contribute significantly to efficiency, safety, and the seamless functioning of operations. The ascent of Blockchain technology is closely intertwined with the emergence of automated procedures known as smart contracts.

Smart contracts serve the purpose of automatically executing agreements, ensuring adherence to contractual terms, minimizing exceptions, and eliminating intermediaries.

However, challenges persist in the realm of blockchain and smart contracts. A primary issue is their detachment from the real world, existing within specific blockchain ecosystems—akin to a siloed or specific truth. A critical missing link is the connection to (off-chain) truth derived from the physical world.

This challenge is concerned with the quality of input data from external souces such as financial market data, weather data, human behaviour data (for example births and deaths) and is commonly referred to as "the oracle problem".[1]

Note

1. The blockchain oracle problem is well explained by the Chainlink Foundation who specialize in providing real-world, off-chain data to blockchains and is paid transaction fees for its services. https://chain.link/education-hub/oracle-problem.

Chapter 8

Kanban

The Japanese word "Kanban" translates to "signboard" or "billboard" in English.

It is a scheduling system originally developed by Toyota in the 1940s as part of their "Lean" Just-in-Time production method.

- *Kanban provides visual clarity and transparency of all transfers, transactions, hand-offs, and changes in ownership (or responsibility).*
- *Kanban facilitates transactions between two or more parties (stakeholders) which have common goals and objectives for the outcomes of the transaction.*

Think of Kanban as traffic flow management. Just as traffic lights and road signs guide vehicles smoothly through intersections, a Kanban system helps to guide tasks and transactions through different transfers and hand-offs.

A Kanban system helps to synchronize tasks and transactions to reduce the waste of waiting and "missed connections".

When a task or transaction is delayed at a particular stage, it is immediately visible, prompting timely intervention to keep the workflow moving. This prevents queues, waiting lines, and backlogs. Kanban also prevents stockouts due to poor management of stock (inventory) levels.

Learning Objectives

Upon completing this chapter, you will be familiar with:

- What is Kanban?

DOI: 10.4324/9781003599715-8

- Examples of Kanban
- A supermarket model
- Kanban digitalization
- Blockchain-based Kanban
- Autonomous supply chains (ASC)

What Is a Kanban ?

Kanban is an enabler for:

- A supermarket model
- A pull system
- System feedback loops
- Just-in-time production
- First-time-right production

Kanban Principles

Kanban gives an obvious (usually visual) signal about:

- **What** needs to be transferred
- **When** it needs to be transferred
- **How** much needs to be transferred
- **Where** it should be transferred

"The job of management is to improve the system".—Taiichi Ohno[1]

Key Benefits of Kanban

- ☐ Reduced waste
- ☐ Improved efficiency
- ☐ Enhanced visibility

☐ Flexibility and adaptability
☐ Better quality control
☐ Increased productivity
☐ Cost reduction
☐ Higher customer satisfaction
☐ Empowered workforce
☐ Enhanced communication
☐ Minimized overburden
☐ Smoother flow
☐ More predictable outcomes
☐ Rapid problem solving
☐ Sustainability

 "Make your workplace a showcase that can be understood by everyone at a glance".
—Taiichi Ohno[2]

Examples of Kanbans

Kanbans come in many forms. For example:

■ A physical card
■ A light
■ A low-level mark on a container
■ A visual alert on a digital monitor (screen)
■ A notification on your mobile phone
■ A binary status indicator, 0 or 1

Hospital Operations

Many hospitals implement Kanban systems to efficiently manage the inventory of medical supplies and medications. These systems either use physical cards or electronic detectors (such as level sensors) to signal when stocks are low and need replenishment, helping to maintain the availability of essential items while avoiding overstocking.

Retail Stores

Retailers use Kanban systems to effectively manage their inventory. When a product is sold, a Kanban signal is sent to reorder the item, ensuring optimal stock levels and minimizing the chances of stockouts or overstocking.

Restaurants

In a restaurant, a Kanban system between the cashier, the waiter, and the cook can enhance efficiency and streamline operations. This can be seen easily in any McDonalds[3] restaurant with the visual displays for both the customers and the kitchen workers.

Courier Delivery Services

The delivery is tracked using a combination of technologies, such as GPS and electronic signatures, providing real-time information on the delivery status to both the customer and the logistics team.

Manufacturing

Kanban cards are attached to bins or containers holding parts. When parts are used, the empty bin and its card signal the need for replenishment.

- Part matching between two machines producing different parts and the "best fit" parts from each machine need to come together
- Notification on your mobile phone that your car is ready for pickup from the garage
- Make a notification that you need more milk

What Is a Supermarket Model?

The phrase "supermarket" is often associated with Kanban. Much of the Kanban system created by Toyota in the 1960s was inspired by the efficiency of the then-popular supermarket chain called "Piggly Wiggly" in the USA.[4]

Just as a supermarket keeps its shelves stocked with just the right amount of products, the supermarket model in manufacturing involves maintaining a designated size of storage space for parts or materials between two successive production stages.

The key concept is that the downstream operation, analogous to a supermarket customer, withdraws parts from this storage space as needed. When **parts** are removed, **a visual signal**, the Kanban, prompts the upstream operation to replenish the stock. This system minimizes excess inventory, reduces lead times, and ensures that resources are used efficiently, ultimately improving the overall production process.

The shipment of a postal package with companies like Amazon utilizes various Kanban-like signals and systems to facilitate the process smoothly and track progress.

Here is an example of how this can work: Online Order.

The process begins when a customer orders the book online. This order is considered the "Kanban signal", marking the starting point of the process.

Order Confirmation

Once the order is placed, the customer receives a confirmation email or message, acting as an electronic Kanban signal to indicate that the order has been received and is being processed.

Preparation and Packaging

In the distribution center, products are gathered and packaged for shipment. During this process, visual signals such as marked floor zones, shelves, or storage bins can be used to specify which products need to be collected for specific orders.

Shipping Status Updates

After the package is dispatched, the customer can receive **status updates** through electronic messages or tracking codes. This serves as a continuous Kanban signal, showing where the package is within the delivery process.

Delivery Confirmation

Once the package is delivered, the customer typically receives a confirmation through an electronic message, which serves as the final Kanban signal to indicate the successful completion of the order.

Kanban principles and signals provide **updates or feedback loops** to track, trace, and optimize the progress of processes. This usually happens for business-to-customer relationships (B2C). We explain why this rarely happens for business-to-business (B2B) relationships in the paragraph "Blockchain Kanban".

Internet: Kanban Digitization of Information

Digitization of Kanban systems rapidly happened with the rise of the internet in the 1990s and the Internet of Things (IoT) in the 2000s. Physical Kanban cards and boards were transformed into digital formats. This provided real-time, automatic communication and status updates.

Some examples of Kanban digitization are:

Digital Kanban Boards

Instead of using physical cards or sticking physical "Post-it" notes on physical boards (whiteboards), teams have transitioned to digital signals, alerts on monitors and screens, and digital Kanban boards.

These digital signals and screens can be accessed from anywhere with an internet connection, making it easy for team members to view and update the status of tasks, transactions, or products.

Notifications and Alerts

When a task or transaction status changes, notifications and alerts can be sent to relevant team members. These notifications can take the form of text messages, mobile app notifications, or email alerts. This ensures that everyone involved is instantly informed of any updates or changes.

Ringtones and Auditory Alerts

In addition to visual notifications, teams can use auditory alerts like ringtones or customized sound cues to grab the attention of team members when an urgent update or change occurs. These sounds can be associated with specific types of updates, helping to distinguish their importance.

Cloud-Based Collaboration Tools

Many cloud-based collaboration tools offer Kanban board features. These tools provide a centralized location for teams to collaborate, manage tasks, and receive real-time updates. They also allow for integration with other software and services.

Internet of Things (IoT) Devices

Internet of Things devices can be used to digitize Kanban processes. For example, sensors can detect the status of physical inventory and trigger notifications or updates automatically when stock levels reach a certain point.

Integration with Other Systems

Digital Kanban systems can be integrated with other software and systems, such as customer relationship management tools or enterprise resource planning systems, to ensure a seamless flow of information and updates across the organization.

Overall, the digitizing of physical Kanbans with internet-driven tools enhances communication, collaboration, and efficiency, enabling teams to manage their workflows more effectively in today's fast-paced, interconnected business environment.

The Key Benefits of Kanban Digitization

- ☐ Real-time information
- ☐ Efficiency and productivity
- ☐ Flexibility
- ☐ User engagement
- ☐ Reminders and follow-ups
- ☐ Convenience and accessibility
- ☐ Personalization
- ☐ Interaction and call-to-action

Blockchain: Kanban Digitalization of Relations

Blockchain technology enables users to share status updates with pseudonymous actors, eliminating the need to rely on any central authority.

The "Who", "When", and "What" of each transaction is stored in a decentralized manner and validated using consensus mechanisms that prevent fraud and "bad actors" from having influence. See Figure 8.1.

This "disintermediation" and "trust by design" allow for a whole new landscape to open up for the use of Kanbans.

Kanbans can now be used between diverse stakeholders in a long supply chain, or even between competitors in the same market who can mutually benefit from knowing certain status updates from each other.

How Does Blockchain Facilitate Kanban Systems?

Blockchain serves as a comprehensive timestamping tool, capturing essential information about the "who, when, what, and why" of transactions and status updates.

By integrating Blockchain technology into Lean Kanban systems, teams can leverage improved visibility, automation, and real-time collaboration. This synergy of Lean principles and blockchain features enables new levels of streamlined and efficient workflow and drives better outcomes for all stakeholders in a system.

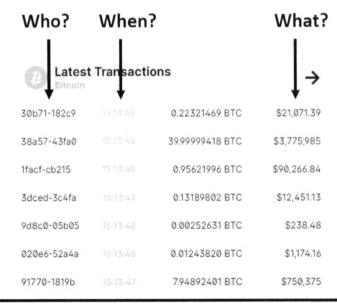

Figure 8.1   A blockchain records the 'Who', the 'When' and the 'What' for every transaction.

Blockchain-Based Kanbans vs Internet-Based Kanbans

Blockchain further facilitates digitization of Kanbans on top of what the internet has already achieved. Let's compare a typical internet-based digital Kanban with a blockchain-based Kanban.

Real-Time Information

Like internet applications, Blockchain technology can deliver real-time notifications that offer immediate, up-to-date information about events, updates, or messages. However, unlike internet notifications, blockchain notifications are both **immutable and programmable**, **with built-in logic**, grounded in business agreements among stakeholders and secured by the highest levels of cryptographic trust "by design".

Efficiency and Productivity

Notifications can enhance efficiency and productivity by keeping users informed about tasks, appointments, deadlines, or new messages. This allows them to respond quickly to important matters and manage their time more effectively.

User Engagement

Notifications help increase user engagement with applications and websites. By receiving relevant and personalized notifications, users feel more connected to the platforms they use.

Trust in Code

Internet-based Kanbans rely on internet connectivity to function. Trust in the system is established through user authentication and the security measures implemented within the internet-based platform. Trust is based on the service provider's infrastructure and protocols.

Blockchain-based Kanbans leverage Blockchain technology, which is a decentralized and immutable ledger. Trust in this system is established through cryptographic consensus and the decentralized nature of blockchain. Transactions and information recorded on the blockchain are highly secure and tamper-resistant.

Accountability

Data on internet-based Kanbans can be altered or deleted by users with the appropriate permissions. While there may be version control and audit trails, data can still be modified by authorized users. This is different with blockchain-based Kanbans.

Once data is recorded on a blockchain, it is nearly impossible to alter or delete.

The immutability of the blockchain ensures that data remains secure and unchangeable, providing a high level of data integrity and trust. Immutability leads to ownership and accountability, especially when combined with the transparency component.

What Is CRUD?

CRUD is an acronym that comes from the world of computer programming and refers to the four functions that are considered necessary to implement a persistent storage application: **Create, Read, Update,** and **Delete.**

The blockchain is designed to be an append-only structure. A user can only add more data in the form of additional blocks. The delete function is missing.

Transparency and Traceability

With internet-based Kanbans, transparency and traceability are reliant on the service provider's policies and practices. Users must trust the provider to maintain a transparent and accountable system. Blockchain's transparent and decentralized nature inherently provides accountability and traceability. All participants can verify and audit the data on the blockchain, ensuring trust based on distributed consensus rather than trust in a single entity.

Security

With internet-based Kanbans, security measures rely on the service provider's infrastructure and practices, which can be vulnerable to breaches or data manipulation. Blockchain's security is based on cryptographic algorithms and decentralization, making it highly resistant to hacking or fraudulent activities. The consensus mechanism adds an additional layer of security.

Integration and Interoperability

With internet-based Kanbans, the integration with other internet-based tools and systems may require custom development and API (Application Programming Interface). Interoperability can be a challenge. Blockchain's modular and open architecture can facilitate easier integration with other blockchain-based systems and applications, improving interoperability.

Data Ownership and Control

With internet-based Kanbans, users typically have limited control over their data. Data is often stored on the service provider's servers. With blockchain-based Kanbans, users have greater control over their data and can maintain ownership. Data stored on the blockchain is distributed, and users can access and manage it directly.

CASE STUDY

Data from physical infrastructure is made more transparent and accessible to all stakeholders using Blockchain technology.

Data can then be used as a Kanban for status and alerts to any organization or person who can benefit from knowing!

Decentralized Physical Infrastructure Networks (De-PIN) represent a shift in how data from infrastructure systems is managed and controlled. The De-PIN utilizes Blockchain technology to decentralize and share data associated with physical infrastructure such as telecommunications and energy distribution systems, but also such things as transport systems and household devices.

Bosch/LEGIC[5]

Bosch/LEGIC released their BOSCH XDK hardware device in 2023 with eight sensors that store data to the Peaq blockchain where it can be viewed and used by anyone who can use the data for their advantage/efficiency (and is prepared to pay fees for its use).

The sensors included in the LEGIC/Bosch XDK are:

■ Accelerometer
■ Gyroscope
■ Magnetometer
■ Humidity sensor
■ Temperature sensor
■ Acoustic sensor
■ Light sensor

The Bosch XDK can capture a wide range of environmental and motion data, making it suitable for various applications in the IoT.

The Future of Kanban: Autonomous Supply Chains

Digital technologies, such as artificial intelligence and predictive algorithms, are increasingly being used in the supply chain domain, automating various processes. However, so far, these automation efforts have mainly focused on individual processes within the silo of one business, with limited sharing of status or cross-silo integration.

The concept of ASC is that supply chains become capable of autonomous learning and decision-making without human intervention.[6]

This version on the supply chain will be interconnected and intelligent. Kanban signals will be generated to give instructions about the correct quantities that need to be moved at the correct times in order to avoid the wastes of over-production, excessive inventories, stockouts, or delays.

Summary

Kanbans add value to users by delivering relevant information, improving efficiency, and increasing engagement in the process to be done. Strategic notification use enhances the user experience and contributes to the success of digital platforms.

The primary difference between internet-based Kanbans and blockchain-based Kanbans is found in their underlying technology, trust frameworks, and the levels of security, accountability, and transparency they offer.

Blockchain-based Kanbans are particularly advantageous in situations where data integrity, security, and decentralization are critical.

The future of blockchain-based Kanbans lies in De-PIN and ASC.

Notes

1. Ohno, T. (1982). *Taiichi Ohno's Workplace Management.*
2. Ohno, T. (1982). *Taiichi Ohno's Workplace Management.*
3. McDonald's Corporation was one of the first restaurant companies to implement Lean principles and Kanban systems to enhance their operations. (Boston University) https://www.bu.edu/bhr/2012/09/01/the-restaurant-as -hybrid-lean-manufacturer-and-service-provider/.
4. Ohno, T. (1988). *Toyota Production System: Beyond Large-Scale Production.*
5. https://www.xdk.io/ LEGIC Identsystems Ltd.
6. Butner, K. (2010). The Smarter Supply Chain of the Future. *Strategy Leadership*, 38(1), 22–31.

Chapter 9

Tokenization

Tokenization is the process whereby ownership and control rights of a physical asset are represented by a digital identity of that asset on a blockchain together with the digital identity of the owner or controller. The tokens created in the tokenization process serve as fundamental building blocks for true digital transformation. Tokenization can be used effectively in the digital transformation of supply chains, manufacturing processes, financial processes, real estate, and insurance. This chapter serves as an introduction to tokenization and its impact on digital transformation across diverse domains.

Learning Objectives

Upon completing this chapter, you will be familiar with:

- Examples of tokens that are not on a blockchain
- What are the Lean benefits and new possibilities of using digital tokens?
- Examples of digital tokens
- The tokenization process
- Why should tokenization be understood by Lean practitioners?
- New Lean ways of process design: "Two choices thinking"
- A Linear economy versus a circular economy
- Decentralized Physical Infrastructure Networks (DePIN) and Real-World Assets (RWA's).

 DOI: 10.4324/9781003599715-9

Examples of Tokens That Are Not on a Blockchain

Although we may not be aware of them, tokens are already widely used in our daily lives. We use physical and internet-based tokens already for proof of ownership, identity, or access, and they play an important role in simplifying processes and facilitating transactions in various domains.

These examples of physical and internet-based tokens assist in many of the principles of Lean methodology, streamlining operations and improving organizational efficiency. In this section, we provide examples of tokens that are already used in our daily lives.

Physical Money

Physical money is the most obvious example of a token. The money itself does not have value; it is what it represents which is important. Money functions as a tangible representation of the intangible concept of value, enabling economic transactions and serving a critical purpose within an economy. As a token, it embodies consensus about value and facilitates the exchange of goods and services within a society.

Debit Card

A debit card can be viewed as a token due to its role in representing access to financial resources and as a means of authentication in financial transactions. You don't have to have physical money in your pocket to make a purchase. The debit card is a token of your ability to exchange money.

Passports and Identity Cards

A passport or identity card is a token representing your actual identity and existence. It assists in providing access and specific privileges associated with international travel and entry across physical borders. Without a passport token or identity card token, do you still exist as a human?…of course you do! Do others in society acknowledge your existence in the same way without your token? Usually, the answer is "No"!

Side-note: The subject of identity is considered in the book "The Invisible Son" by Tey El-Rjula.[1]

Tey suggests that "no one" is safe from the danger of losing their identity and demonstrates how technology can be used for good.

Tickets for Access

Tickets as a token represent permission or rights for access to events (concerts, films, sports matches), travel (train, bus, or plane tickets) or services.

Postage Stamps

The use of postage stamps is a token of proof of payment to physically deliver something from one party to another party.

Access Cards: With or Without a Near Field Communication Embedded Device

These tokens represent specific authorization or permission to access certain areas like offices, buildings, or events.

Membership Cards

These tokens signify belonging to a particular group, club, or organization and often grant access to exclusive services, discounts, or privileges.

Keys

A physical key is a physical token for access control to homes, vehicles, lockers, etc.

QR Codes and Barcodes

QR code and barcodes are tokens which represent information linked to products, tickets, or services and are scanned to access or obtain specific rights or information.

Vouchers and Gift Cards

Vouchers and gift cards are tokens that represent to the owner a certain value or credit for specific goods or services and can be redeemed accordingly.

Loyalty Cards and Points Cards

Loyalty cards or points cards are tokens which represent accumulated points or rewards based on purchases or activities and can be redeemed for discounts, free items, or other benefits.

Smart Cards

Smart cards such as public transport cards or prepaid cards are tokens that store monetary value or access rights electronically.

Raffle Tickets and Lottery Tickets

Raffle tickets and lottery tickets are tokens which represent a chance or probability to win a prize in a drawing or lottery.

Tokens in Board Games or Arcades

Board game or arcade game tokens are used to play games, access specific features, or provide rewards within a gaming environment. Poker chips in a casino are a good example of this category of token.

Figure 9.1   Permission from the International Lean Six Sigma Institute, ILSSI, Cambridge, UK.

Credentials or Certificates

Validation and authentication of qualifications, skills, or achievements in education, professional fields, or training programs is achieved using the token of a physical or digital certificate. This has been done since the earliest days of education as a reward for study and acknowledgment of achievement. See the example of certification use for Lean Management issued by the International Lean Six Sigma Institute, Cambridge, UK (See figure 9.1).

Coupons

Shopping coupons are tokens that represent discounts or offers for specific products or services.

Wristbands and Hand Stamps

Wristbands and hand stamps are popular tokens used in events or festivals to grant access or indicate admission.

Stickers and Labels

Stickers and Labels as tokens can signify authenticity, expiration dates, or specific information on products or items.

Most commonly tokens are representations of **ownership and rights**. They align with Lean principles by enhancing visibility, streamlining processes, improving accountability, and facilitating continuous improvement efforts within an organization's operations. This last section explored physical and internet-based token examples. Why are digital tokens stored on a blockchain different and superior to physical and internet-based tokens?

What Are the Lean Benefits of Using Tokens?

Improved efficiency is the goal of most organizations, to optimize processes, reduce errors, and improve communication, collaboration, and cooperation. A powerful tool to achieve these goals is the use of digital tokens. These simple yet effective representations of physical assets can help to optimize many aspects of business operations, from verifying identity to tracking customer behavior. Let's take a look at how tokens are revolutionizing Lean practices, delivering benefits ranging from visual clarity, improved flow, identifying improvement opportunities, and reduction of waste.

Simplification

Tokens simplify processes by reducing the need for verbal or written communication to convey ownership, control, or access. For example, instead of verifying someone's identity with a human interaction (visual verification), a digital passport token or ID card token can quickly and effectively provide the necessary information.

Visual Representation

Digital or physical tokens can provide a visual representation of ownership, access, or value of any intangible asset.

For example:

■ Such as "Platinum level" frequent flyer status for a passenger of airline
■ The "Star Rating" of a restaurant or hotel

- Poker or Blackjack chips in a casino effectiveness of a "social influencer"
- The stamps on a card each time you buy a coffee, which can be redeemed for a free coffee

This visualization of something that is intangible or subjective makes it easy to identify, control, and manage the asset or item of value. and manage the asset.

This visual clarity helps in decision-making and in organizing and controlling the asset efficiently, reducing errors and misunderstandings.

Standardization

Tokens can represent standardized units of value or access, promoting consistency and uniformity in transactions.

This standardization **reduces variability** and ensures **predictability** in processes, contributing to overall **efficiency and reduction of errors.**

Improved Flow

Tokens facilitate the smooth flow of activities by ensuring that resources are allocated appropriately to their control and management. Lean principles teach us that inappropriate resource allocation is one of the biggest reasons for poor flow. Tokens facilitate the smooth flow of activities by ensuring appropriate resource allocation, preventing bottlenecks, queues, and delays.

Ease of Communication

Using digital tokens that represent key concepts or components facilitate communication and understanding among teams or individuals, allowing for quicker decision-making and problem-solving.

Continuous Improvement

Tokens can also serve as a means of collecting data for process analysis and better understanding of processes for improvement opportunities. For example, tokenized membership cards can track customer behavior and preferences, enabling organizations to adjust and optimize their products and services more effectively.

Overall, the use of tokens in Lean practices can simplify processes, enhance visual management, standardize operations, improve flow, facilitate communication, and support continuous improvement efforts, reducing unwanted variation and waste in processes.

Tokenization of Real-World Assets to Create Tokens on a Blockchain

Tokenization with Blockchain technology involves producing a digital fingerprint of an RWA combined with the digital fingerprint of the current owner or controller, and storing the digital information on a blockchain. The tokens can represent multiple different asset types, such as physical goods, financial instruments, intellectual property, identity, data, or intangible assets such as entry rights, benefits, and privileges.

This concept of moving from the "it", such as a tree, to the digital fingerprint stored on a blockchain in "bits" is illustrated in Figure 9.2.

Digital Twins

A token can also represent a "digital twin" of a tangible and non-tangible asset. The term "digital twin" is commonly used in smart manufacturing, smart factories[2], and supply chains.

Tokenization of Achievements

Each academic achievement (like grades, certificates, and diplomas) can be represented as a token on the blockchain. This ensures the records are immutable and easily verifiable.

Figure 9.2 The move from the "It" to the "Bit"!

By creating this token there is no need for physical documents; it prevents fraud and simplifies the verification process for employers or other institutions.

Track and Trace Functionality

Tokens can be used to record attendance. Each class or event attended could generate a token that is added to the student's blockchain profile.

Motivation

Students could earn tokens for participation or achievements, which can be redeemed for rewards or recognition.

Payments with Tokens

Payments could be made using cryptocurrency tokens, simplifying international transactions, and reducing fees.

Peer-to-Peer Transactions

Student Marketplace: Students can use tokens for buying and selling books, notes, or other items directly with each other.

Example Scenario

Imagine a university is implementing a blockchain system for student management. Here's a simplified example of how it works for a student named Ivan.

Enrollment

Ivan enrolls in a new course, and a smart contract issues him a course token.

Attendance

Every time Ivan attends a lecture, a token is recorded on the blockchain to mark his attendance.

Assignments and Exams

When Ivan submits an assignment or takes an exam, his performance is recorded as tokens on the blockchain.

Grades

At the end of the semester, his grades are tokenized and added to his academic record on the blockchain. Upon graduation, Ivan receives a digital diploma in the form of a token, which he can share with potential employers for verification.

What Are the Lean Benefits and New Possibilities of Digital Tokens Stored on a Blockchain?

The advent of digital tokens on a blockchain offers new Lean benefits and transformative possibilities.

Blockchain enabled tokenization represents **a paradigm shift** in the way assets are owned, traded, and managed. By using Blockchain technology, digital tokens offer numerous benefits that fit seamlessly with Lean principles. From streamlining asset ownership processes to promoting transparency and security, the Lean benefits of digital tokens are multifaceted and far-reaching.

The symbiotic relationship between Lean methodologies and digital tokenization on blockchains is an innovative approach that not only optimizes workflows, but also opens new ways for improving efficiency, accessibility, and financial markets. Through a lens of Lean thinking, we explore how blockchain enabled tokenization revolutionizes value co-creation, reduces costs, increases flexibility, and democratizes investment opportunities, improving the whole instead of its parts. Let's start with the Lean benefits of tokenization on a blockchain:

Streamlining and Optimization

Blockchain enabled tokenization streamlines asset ownership processes, promoting alignment, efficiency, accountability, and transparency across the entire workflow. This resonates with Lean System Thinking, emphasizing process optimization, collaborative synergy, waste reduction, and positive impacts on both customers and the environment.

Systems Value Stream Mapping

In Lean methodologies, value stream mapping is a tool used to identify areas for improvement within a system. Blockchain enabled tokenization improves this process by clearly delineating the flow of asset ownership, allowing for in-depth analysis and optimization.

Reduced Overheads

Blockchain enabled tokenization removes the need for intermediaries and reduces transaction costs, aligning with Lean's goals. It facilitates efficient communication and information sharing enhancing process organizational effectiveness. compared to existing structures.

Flexibility and Adaptability

Blockchain enabled tokenization's fractional ownership and trade simplicity offer financial investment flexibility. It facilitates adaptability in asset ownership and investment, aligning with Lean's ethos of agile and flexible adaptation to market and environmental changes.

Accessibility and Risk Management

Blockchain enabled tokenization democratizes investment opportunities, allowing small investors to participate in markets that were previously inaccessible to them. Where investing in real estate, for example, was previously only reserved for the rich, tokenization also makes this accessible to less wealthy people. It also reduces the risk of investment by sharing ownership and accountability.

Market Liquidity

Non-liquid assets such as real estate and private equity can become more liquid through blockchain tokenization, enhancing market liquidity and potentially reducing risks associated with these assets.

Transparency and Security

Blockchain-based tokenization provides transparent and secure transaction histories, reducing fraud, and ensuring the integrity of ownership records.

Incentives and Responsibilities: "Skin in the Game" Processes

Blockchain-based tokenization creates "skin in the game" processes by promoting a system of incentives, responsibilities, and governance structures that encourage active participation, fairness, and collaboration among network participants.

What Are the New Possibilities with Digital Tokens?

The blockchain-based tokenization of ownership offers many new possibilities. In Figure 9.3 below we show some of them.

- Blockchain-based tokenization broadens access to investment opportunities, facilitating *interoperability*, and increasing *liquidity* in markets.
- Blockchain-based tokenization enables *fractional ownership of assets* in traditionally illiquid markets such as real estate, allowing broader *participation and diversification.*

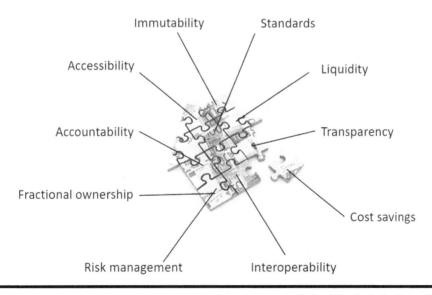

Figure 9.3   Some of the many new possibilities presented by blockchain-based tokenization of ownership.

■ Blockchain-based tokenization provides a *transparent*, secure, and *auditable transaction history*, ensuring *trust* and *accountability* within the system.

■ Blockchain-based tokenization enables traceability of materials, products, or services, vital for creating a **circular, regenerative**, and *accountable economy.*

■ Blockchain-based tokenization enables collaboration on *shared purposes* with *standardized processes.*

■ Blockchain-based tokenization results in immutable tokens that cannot be destroyed or altered. This enables lifecycle management of assets, ensuring *reliable and unalterable* records throughout the life of the token.

Tokenized-asset: A digital representation of value or rights which can be transferred and stored electronically using blockchain distributed ledger technology. For example, a token can represent ownership of a physical shoe or t-shirt, or the right to use a bicycle.

Input → Token → Output

As Blockchain technology tokenization and cryptocurrencies continue to grow and evolve, there are more and more interesting use-cases being developed.

Examples:

■ Blockchain-based tokens for providing priority levels to autonomous vehicles. Which vehicle goes first at a junction when both arrive at the same time?

■ Parking tokens owned by the vehicle and not the driver.

■ Security tokens for passing through priority gates at a concert or sports event.

Categories of Blockchain-Based Tokens

Several different categories of blockchain-based tokens have been developed since the genesis of blockchains. Each token is subject to different rules (protocols), responsibilities, and functionalities depending on their classification. In this exploration, we examine the diversity of tokens, with different categories offering unique characteristics, serving different purposes and with different use-cases.

The token category can also determine the extent of external regulation, control, and ability to conform to legal requirements. Different tokens are subject to varying regulations, duty of care, and specific rules of conduct based on what is being tokenized.

Here's a brief explanation of different types of tokens:

Security Tokens

Security tokens represent ownership in an asset, similar to traditional securities like stocks or bonds. They are regulated and typically offer rights to dividends, profit shares, or voting rights within a company. Security tokens must comply with securities regulations.

For example, a security token might represent ownership in a real estate property or shares in a company. An example is the tokenization of shares in a startup, where investors receive tokens representing their ownership stake.

Utility Tokens

Utility tokens provide access rights to a product or service within a particular platform or ecosystem. They're not designed as investments but rather as a means of accessing specific functionalities or services. These tokens are often used to pay for goods or services within a specific ecosystem (for example the Cosmos[3] ecosystem or the Polkadot[4] ecosystem).

An example would be Ethereum's Ether, which is used to pay for transaction fees and smart contract execution within the Ethereum network (the second largest blockchain).

Equity Token

Equity tokens represent ownership in a company, similar to traditional stocks. They grant rights to dividends, voting, and other ownership privileges. These tokens differ from security tokens as they may not always fall under strict regulatory oversight.

An example could be a tokenized representation of shares in a private company.

Asset Token

Asset tokens represent ownership or rights to physical or digital assets such as commodities, art, or intellectual property. These tokens enable fractional ownership or trade of these assets on a blockchain.

For instance, a piece of art could be tokenized, allowing investors to buy and trade fractions of this art object. You could charge people an entrance fee to have a look at the object, which in turn generates (fractionized) passive income for you.

Reward and Incentivization Tokens

These tokens reward and incentivize certain behaviors or actions within an ecosystem or community. They can be earned through participation, contribution, or specific achievements, and often signify reputation or value within a community.

An example is Steem's token, STEEM[5], which rewards users for creating and curating content on the Steem blockchain-based social media platform.

These tokens demonstrate diverse functionalities and purposes within the blockchain and crypto space, each catering to different aspects of ownership, utility, incentives, or rewards within their respective ecosystems.

This diverse landscape of these tokens underlines both the complexity and the potential opportunities of Blockchain technology.

Two Choices Thinking: From Transferring the Whole to Transferring the Goal

Imagine you are playing a really simple game with your friend. You can only ask questions that have a "Yes" or "No" answer. You get only one piece of information returned to you.

We can call this **one "bit" of information**.

In the world of computers, everything works in "bits". **A bit is the smallest unit of information a computer can handle**[6]. It's the building block of all digital data.

When you ask a "Yes" or "No" question in the computer world, it's represented by either a 0 or a 1.

A "Yes" might be represented by a 1.

A "No" might be represented by a 0.

Imagine checking a young person's age for entry into a bar or night-club. Instead of sharing all the information, the exact date of birth, the system can simply provide a "Yes" or "No" answer to the question whether the person is over 18 years old. This produces a "bit" as either a 1 or a 0. Zero knowledge (ZK[7]) is transferred about the exact date of birth, the name of the person, or any other information. Only the answer to the specific question is given.

Figure 9.4   Blockchain for proof of age without giving away other information such as name or address.

In this process design **the full information is not shared; only the answer to the question is shared**. This has several advantages:

Privacy Protection

Sharing only "yes" or "no" answers minimizes the amount of sensitive information exposed. This helps with GDPR (General Data Protection Regulation)[8] compliance, as only the necessary information is shared and/or stored.

Simplicity

The process becomes simpler and more efficient because less data is exchanged and processed. This can lead to faster verifications and transactions.

Transparency and Trust

Because only the necessary information is shared, the process is allowed to become more transparent, and trust can be established between parties more easily. It is not necessary to trust the other party with more information than they need. This contributes to a better user experience and customer satisfaction.

Compliance

By complying with GDPR (General Data Protection Regulations)[9], organizations can avoid fines and legal complications arising from improper handling of privacy data.

Conclusion

Using **status updates** in the form of "yes" or "no" answers can be an effective way to protect privacy-sensitive information while still providing needed functionality. This new process design can help create safer, more efficient, and compliant systems.

Tokenization transforms "ITs" (identities, objects) into BITs (digital representation). Any physical identity (IT) can have a digital representation on the Internet (BIT). With smart process designs we can get answers to questions without having to share unnecessary information and knowledge. We can give an answer (in order to prove something) without also giving additional knowledge about the answer (this is also known as a ZK proof[10]).

Welcome to the world of programmable internet!

Why Should Tokenization Be Understood by Lean Practitioners and Consultants?

Lean practitioners and consultants should embrace the evolving potential of blockchain-based tokenization. This technology introduces new value propositions, motivational and incentive techniques for optimizing processes. The value of Lean has advanced beyond mere process improvement to now including ways to develop community values such as inclusivity, biodiversity, sustainability, and other social challenges.

Here are some examples of community values and sustainable goals that can be improved using blockchain-based tokenization with Lean principles:

1. *Accelerating Financing of the Circular Economy in Climate and Biodiversity Strategies*

Financing the circular economy is a challenge in our contemporary financial framework. Using blockchain-based tokenization helps to propel financial support towards sustainable practices that support **resource efficiency, minimize waste, and promote environmental preservation**.

Embracing the circular economy within climate and biodiversity strategies presents an opportunity to drive impactful change by aligning financial investments with the principles of sustainability and ecological balance. What are the building blocks for financing in this new framework?

■ Crowd Funding and Sourcing

Blockchain technology offers an innovative way to bring people together and raise funds for common goals, such as accelerating financing for the circular economy within climate and biodiversity strategies. Blockchain enables individuals and organizations to unite in a very fast way, raise funds, and collaborate towards a more sustainable future.

■ Supply Chain Transparency

Blockchain enables transparent and immutable recording of transactions, providing a comprehensive view of the entire supply chain. This transparency is crucial for verifying the authenticity and sustainability of products, ensuring they meet green and clean standards. Consumers can trace the origin, journey, and environmental impact of goods, encouraging the adoption of eco-friendly practices.

■ Provenance and Authentication

Blockchain can trace and authenticate the origin (provenance) of raw materials, ensuring they come from sustainable sources. This feature helps in combating counterfeit products and ensures that the materials and people used in the production of goods comply with ethical and environmental standards.

■ Smart Contracts for Sustainability Initiatives

Smart contracts embedded in blockchain can automate and enforce sustainability agreements, ensuring compliance with environmental regulations. For instance, these contracts could automate payments for carbon credits, renewable energy certificates, or other sustainability-related incentives based on predefined criteria.

■ Renewable Energy Trading

Blockchain facilitates peer-to-peer energy trading in microgrids, allowing individuals or businesses to buy and sell excess renewable energy directly, promoting a cleaner energy ecosystem.

■ Carbon Footprint Tracking

Blockchain-based systems can track and manage carbon footprints across the entire lifecycle of products. This enables companies to measure and reduce their carbon emissions, promoting cleaner production processes.

Even more important than capturing and tracking CO_2 and Carbon is the new process design that uses much less CO_2 and Carbon, thanks to peer-to-peer process design.

This tackles the source root cause, instead of monitoring the externalities.

■ Tokenization for Green Investments

Blockchain-based tokens can represent investments and incentives for renewable energy projects or sustainable initiatives. This encourages funding for green projects by providing a transparent and accessible investment platform.

■ Decentralized Governance for Environmental Policies

Blockchain can support decentralized governance models for environmental policies and initiatives. The decentralized consensus protocols of blockchain allow multiple stakeholders to participate in decision-making processes, enabling consensus and effective collaboration towards sustainability goals.

Blockchain technology can help to enhance efforts towards creating clean, green, sustainable, and resilient goods and services. The transparency, traceability, and automation offered by Blockchain technology can significantly contribute to sustainable practices and the development of a more environmentally conscious economy.

2. Bending Our Linear Economy Into a Circular Economy

Tokenization plays a pivotal role in transitioning from a linear to a circular economy, promoting resource efficiency, sustainability, and material reuse. It enables the seamless integration of environmental, social, and governance (ESG) standards into business practices and investment strategies.

The internet of Web 2.0 lacks a **decentralized trust infrastructure** necessary for ensuring collaboration integrity, ethics, and efficiency in shared networks.

Blockchain technology, Web 3.0, offers transparent and immutable transaction records, empowering network participants and stakeholders in the entire end-to-end value stream. This inclusive approach allows participants to hold shares (trust tokens) in each other, aligning individual success with the collective success of the network.

Moreover, tokenization significantly enhances the verification of ESG[11] data. By tracing and validating data origins (provenance), blockchain-based tokenization ensures authenticity and credibility, thereby strengthening the reliability and integrity of ESG information for informed and accurate decision-making.

Especially with the rapid rise of artificial intelligence (AI), it is important to know the origin of data.

Here's How Tokenization Contributes to a Circular System Approach

Asset Fractionalization and Ownership

Blockchain-based tokenization allows for the representation of ownership of physical assets, such as materials, products, or equipment, in a digital form. This facilitates fractional ownership, enabling multiple stakeholders to share resources, encouraging collective responsibility, traceability, and reducing resource waste.

Traceability and Transparency

Tokens on a blockchain can track the journey of materials or products throughout their lifecycle. This transparency ensures visibility into the sourcing, manufacturing, usage, and disposal of goods. It assists in identifying inefficiencies and areas for improvement in the circular flow of resources.

Tokenized Incentives

Tokens on a blockchain can serve as incentives for recycling, reusing, or returning products at the end of their lifecycle. Manufacturers can issue tokens to consumers who return used products, encouraging participation in circular economy practices.

 PlasticBank[12] is a plastic offset program that rewards people with tokens or fiat for collecting plastic waste and taking it to recycling centers. This program is currently running in Haiti, the Philippines, Brazil, and South Africa,

From Software as a Service Towards Blockchain as a Service

Blockchain-based tokenization as a service can support innovative business models, such as product-as-a-service, where ownership remains with the manufacturer and consumers pay for the use of the product. Tokens can represent access rights to the product, usage time, or subscription to services associated with the product, encouraging and incentivizing manufacturers to design products for durability, sustainability, and recyclability.

 Akash[13] Network is an example of an open-source supercloud that allows users to securely and efficiently buy and sell computing resources. It enables users to own their cloud infrastructure, deploy applications, and rent unused cloud resources.

Resource Management and Efficiency

Blockchain-based tokens facilitate the sharing and exchange of resources, equipment, or facilities among businesses or individuals. This sharing economy model optimizes resource utilization, reducing the need for excessive production and consumption.

Verification of Sustainable Practices

Blockchain-based tokens can represent certifications or standards for sustainable practices. For example, tokens can validate eco-friendly materials or production methods, building trust, and incentivizing adherence to circular economy principles.

 The IXO[14] Protocol introduces a groundbreaking standard for creating **Verifiable Impact Claims**, which assess and document the impact of individuals and organizations on global conditions. These claims undergo rigorous evaluation by trusted **Prediction Oracle** services, resulting in the issuance of Impact Proofs and certified digital credentials. These digital assets, certified and validated, serve as modern replacements or improvements to traditional instruments such as verified emission reduction certificates.

Community Engagement and Collaboration

Blockchain-based tokenization enables decentralized collaboration and governance. The tokens can incentivize community participation in circular economy initiatives, promoting collective action and innovation towards sustainable practices.

Decentralized Physical Infrastructure Networks and Real-World Assets

Decentralized Physical Infrastructure Networks and RWAs are an emerging trend within the blockchain sector. These concepts open up a range of new possibilities when ownership of physical assets (RWAs) is placed "on-chain" (on a blockchain).

Access to these assets becomes easier and the fractionalization of these assets leads to new business models, new incentive models, and new markets.

Through token incentives individuals are motivated to contribute to the network. The goal is to offer an alternative to centralized (WEB2-based) applications and compete with the large multinational Web 2 infrastructure-based companies such as Google and Amazon. The DePIN can provide more efficient, resilient and fair alternatives to centralized physical infrastructure networks.

Let's have a look at some existing projects that are already using these concepts and technologies.

The Helium Network[15] is changing the game when it comes to wireless connections. Instead of relying on expensive infrastructure or energy-intensive technologies, Helium offers a decentralized solution that lets devices from anywhere in the world connect to the Internet. This means you can use your phone, laptop, or any other device without needing to be near a Wi-Fi hotspot or a cell tower.

How does it work? Well, it's all thanks to Blockchain technology and a special currency called Helium tokens. These tokens create a marketplace where people who provide wireless coverage can earn money, and those who need to connect their devices can do so at a much lower cost. Helium also provides the tools for developers to easily create devices that use less power and stay connected to the Internet, making it easier than ever to build smart gadgets and connect them to the web.

Hivemapper[16] is creating a super up-to-date map of the world, and they are doing it with the help of regular people like you and me who drive around. Here is how it works: If you have a special dashcam in your car, you can earn rewards, called HONEY, for providing high-quality pictures of the roads you drive on. Then, clever AI technology looks at these pictures and figures out what's in them, like signs, buildings, and other important stuff.

Companies or organizations that need access to this detailed map can buy credits to use Hivemapper's tools. With already over 100 million kilometers of roads mapped in more than 90 countries, including 6 million unique roads, Hivemapper is becoming the go-to for accurate, up-to-date maps all around the world.

DIMO[17] is an open and user-owned network. This means that when businesses use your data, you save time and money while earning rewards. It's a driver's network that's powering the future of mobility. You can share your data on your terms and be rewarded in the long term.

Drivers all over the world are already connected to the network. Enterprises can easily offer services to these cars by tapping into the same protocol, rewards, and user base.

Filecoin[18] is like the Airbnb of data storage. It's a decentralized network where people with extra storage space on their computers can rent it out to others who need to store files securely. Instead of relying on big companies like Amazon or Google for cloud storage, Filecoin allows individuals to make money by renting out their unused disk space.

Users pay for storage using Filecoin, a cryptocurrency specifically designed for the network. This system ensures that files are stored securely across a distributed network of computers, making it more dependable and resistant to censorship or data loss.

Theta Network[19] is like a supercharged version of Netflix or YouTube, but with a twist—it's powered by Blockchain technology and its own special token.

Here's how it works:

Firstly, the network uses these tokens to encourage regular people like you and me to share our extra computer power and internet bandwidth. This helps make streaming videos smoother and faster, especially when you are watching high-quality content like 4K or 8K videos.

Imagine if, instead of just relying on big, expensive servers in one location, your video could be streamed from multiple places closer to you. That's the idea behind Theta Network—it solves the "last-mile" problem by using these shared resources to deliver videos more efficiently.

But it's not just about making things faster and cheaper for video platforms. By rewarding people with tokens for sharing their resources, Theta Network also gives viewers like us a reason to engage more with the content. And for video platforms, this means they can attract more viewers, make more money, and stand out from the competition.

Peaq[20] democrats abundance in the age of automation
Imagine a world where everyone, not just the privileged few, benefits from the incredible advancements in technology. That's the vision of Peaq.

As automation and AI become more prevalent, they're transforming industries and taking over tasks that were once done by humans. But instead of fearing job loss, Peaq sees this as an opportunity for everyone to thrive.

On Peaq, the more value these AI-powered machines create, and the more jobs they automate, the more rewards are distributed to everyone. It's about democratizing abundance—ensuring that the benefits of technological progress are shared by all, not just a select few.

So how does Peaq achieve this?

By creating a decentralized digital infrastructure—a sort of global computer—where anyone can build and own apps. These apps can be used to harness the power of machines across various domains, from land to sea, sky, and even space.

Think of it as a community-driven network where people come together to build apps that serve their needs and interests. Whether it's apps for vehicles, robots, or other devices, Peaq provides the tools and platform to make it happen. And because the network is owned and governed by the community, the value generated by these apps is shared among its members.

In essence, Peaq is not just about building technology—it's about building a future where technology serves everyone, empowering communities to thrive in the age of automation.

Summary

Tokenization based on Blockchain technology creates an efficient and transparent framework that aligns with Lean principles, facilitating the shift from linear to circular economies. It enhances resource efficiency, promotes traceability, and fosters collaboration among stakeholders to drive sustainability.

For Lean consultants, comprehending tokenization's impact on ESG goals is critical. It aligns with Lean principles of process optimization, innovation, and sustainability.

Understanding tokenization using Blockchain technology enables effective resource management, strategic decision-making, and the delivery of comprehensive sustainable practices for all organizations.

Notes

1. El-Rjula, T. (2021). The Invisible Son.
2. TWI. What Is a Smart Factory? (A Complete Guide). https://www.twi-global .com/technical-knowledge/faqs/what-is-a-smart-factory.
3. Cosmos. The Internet of Blockchains. https://cosmos.network/.
4. Polkadot. Web3 Interoperability. Decentralized Blockchain. https://polkadot. network/.
5. Steem. Powering Communities and Opportunities. https://steem.com/.
6. Wikipedia. Bit. https://en.wikipedia.org/wiki/Bit.
7. Zero-Knowledge Proofs. https://ethereum.org/en/zero-knowledge-proofs/.
8. Gov.uk. Data Protection: The Data Protection Act. https://www.gov.uk/data -protection.
9. New General Data Protection Regulation (AVG) in EU. https://www.amsadvo-caten.com/blog/intellectual-property-law-in-the-netherlands/are-you-ready-for -the-new-general-data-protection-regulation-avg/.
10. Zero-Knowledge Proofs.https://ethereum.org/en/zero-knowledge-proofs/.
11. Wikipedia. Environmental, Social, and Governance. https://en.wikipedia.org/ wiki/Environmental,_social,_and_governance.
12. Plastic Bank.. Empowering the World to Stop Ocean Plastic. https://plasticbank .com/.
13. Akash Network. Decentralized Compute Marketplace. https://akash.network/.
14. IOX Protocol. The Internet of Impacts. https://www.ixo.world/.
15. Helium. Introducing the People's Network. https://www.helium.com/.
16. Hivemapper. Get Rewarded for Road Mapping. https://www.hivemapper.com/ explorer.
17. DIMO. Connect Your Car and Earn Rewards. https://dimo.zone/.
18. A Decentralized Storage Network for the World's Information. https://filecoin .io/.
19. Theta Network Blockchain Decentralized Cloud for AI, Media & Entertainment. https://www.thetatoken.org/.
20. Peaq. The Blockchain for Real-World Applications. https://www.peaq.network/.

Chapter 10

DMAIC

Achieving operational excellence in any organization requires a methodical and systematic approach to problem-solving and continuous improvement.

In the context of Lean Blockchain System Thinking, the DMAIC (Define, Measure, Analyze, Improve, Control) framework is an excellent tool for providing such a structured approach to improvement.

This chapter begins with an understanding of the DMAIC framework and the Define, Measure, Analyze, Improve and Control phases. By the end of this chapter, readers will appreciate the benefits of DMAIC and understand its application in the transformation from traditional siloed business systems, full of waste and bottlenecks...to connected business systems based on Lean, Blockchain technology and System Thinking.

The framework of DMAIC was proposed and used by Motorola Corporation in 1985, expanded worldwide by General Electric in the 1990's[1], and made popular for use in the service sector by Michael L. George's book *Lean Six Sigma for Service*[2].

Learning Objectives

Upon completing this chapter, readers will:

- Understand the "what" and the "why" of the DMAIC framework
- Understand "how" to use the Define, Measure, and Analyze phase to recognize and understand existing problems and their root causes

in traditional organization (TRAD-ORG) current-state systems and structures

■ Explore the concept of *Innovative Problem Solving* and *Design Thinking* as important tools for the development of solutions during the "Improve" phase of DMAIC

■ Reveal the improved *future-state* of decentralized organizations (DE-ORG), in which removal of silos and peer-to-peer flow of trusted information leads to 10x + efficiencies in throughput (transactions of value) and significant waste reduction

■ Appreciate that DMAIC provides the ideal framework to facilitate this move from "TRAD-ORG" to "DE-ORG"

Introduction

In the previous Cause and Effect chapter, we exposed the inherent problems of our traditional organizational structures (TRAD-ORG), exposing them to generating waste, restricting the flow of value, and providing poor quality outcomes by design. To assist in resolving such problems, we present our adapted DMAIC scheme for Lean Blockchain System Thinking.
See Figure 10.1.

Our thesis is that Blockchain technology and Systems Thinking, supplementing existing Lean principles, will help to improve our organizational structures through improved collaboration, cooperation, and communication, resulting in improved flow of products, information, and payments (PIP

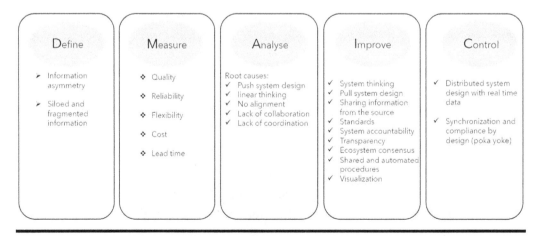

Figure 10.1   Adapted DMAIC scheme for Lean Blockchain System Thinking.

3-flow synchronization[3]), increasing the throughput of value and quality of outcomes.

The maternity healthcare scenario (introduced in Chapter 4) illustrates the inefficiencies embedded in our traditional organizational TRAD-ORG model.

A complex administrative settlement process, involving multiple non-value-added steps and a 90-day payment term, reflects the lack of collaboration and poor synchronization within the system.

It is clear that the TRAD-ORG structure leads to long waiting times, high costs, and low satisfaction for everyone involved.

Define, Measure, and Analyze phases of DMAIC reveal the root causes of inefficiencies within our TRAD-ORG l model.

Two critical issues, **information asymmetry and fragmented/siloed organizational structures,** are discovered to be root causes in TRAD-ORG models and are alone responsible for a substantial proportion of the inefficiencies[4].

Information asymmetry, common in the healthcare process, results in delays and errors, increasing complexity (chaos) and stakeholder dissatisfaction.

The design of solutions to root causes in the "Improve" phase is based on the simple IFTTT[5] (If This Then That) conditional logic protocol.

This protocol lays the foundation for collaborative efforts, emphasizing the "who," "what," and "when" aspects essential to sharing information in an efficient manner.

In the Improvement phase, we can also introduce the 3-flow "Product-Information-Payment" (PIP) Synchronization value-stream model. The 3-flow synchronization removes bottlenecks to create a greater flow of value and less waste.

The improvements also draw upon Lean concepts such as the "supermarket" inventory management system, kanban, standard work, and the creation of one-piece-flow.

The use of innovative problem-solving and design thinking can leverage the transformative potential of Blockchain technology.

Blockchain's control elements, such as consensus, provenance, immutability, feedback loops, transparency, and automated procedures (smart contracts), are improvements as we move from TRAD-ORG to DE-ORG for increasing accountability, trust, integrity, and value...and reducing waiting, costs, and errors.

Define → Measure → Analyze → Improve → Control

The DMAIC framework is used in Lean and Six Sigma methodologies for process improvement. DMAIC stands for Define, Measure, Analyze, Improve, and Control.

Here is a brief explanation of each phase:

■ **Define**
  – Objective: Clearly define the problem, the project goals, and customer (internal and external) requirements.
  – Activities: Develop a project charter, map out the process, identify key stakeholders, and define the scope and objectives.

■ **Measure**
  – Objective: Quantify the problem and establish baseline measurements.
  – Activities: Collect relevant data on current processes, establish key performance metrics, and ensure data accuracy and reliability.

■ **Analyze**
  – Objective: Identify the root causes of the problem.
  – Activities: Analyze the data collected, perform root cause analysis using tools like Fishbone diagrams or Pareto charts, and identify patterns or variations in the process.

■ **Improve**
  – Objective: Develop and implement solutions to address the root causes.
  – Activities: Brainstorm potential solutions, test and validate these solutions through pilot runs or simulations, and implement the most effective changes.

■ **Control**
  – Objective: Ensure that the improvements are sustained over time.
  – Activities: Develop and implement monitoring plans, establish control systems, document new procedures, and train staff to maintain the improvements.

By following the DMAIC framework, organizations can systematically improve processes, eliminate inefficiencies, and enhance overall performance. In this chapter we will use the framework to demonstrate the benefits of using Blockchain technology and System Thinking into Lean management and Lean System Thinking.

In our previous chapter, Cause and Effect, we discovered two critical problems in our traditional organizational model:

1. **Information Silos:** Information is not shared effectively, leading to numerous non-value-adding activities.
2. **Fragmented Organizational Design:** The organizational design is siloed and fragmented, resulting in a lack of alignment and accountability with the overall purpose of the network.

Information asymmetry, where one party has access to different information than the other (or at various times), introduces a layer of confusion and waste within our healthcare process. This inequality is evident and visible on many levels. Asymmetry is the enemy of the shared purpose and aligned activities. See Figure 10.2.

For example, once the maternity nurse finalizes the timesheet, the process undergoes verification and authorization by the parents. However, this action remains isolated from the maternity care agency and the insurer, creating a "black spot" and an information asymmetry.

Several factors can contribute to information asymmetry and siloed and fragmented information:

■ **Lack of Shared Purpose and Alignment**
There is no coordination between the purpose of the total process, the value-adding activities, and how collaboration can be coordinated most effectively.

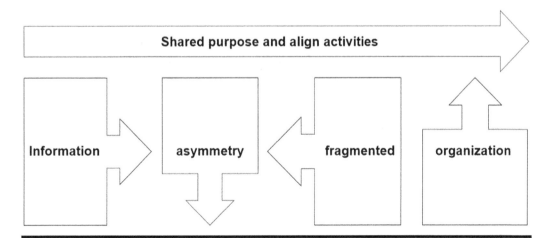

Figure 10.2   Asymmetry is the enemy of the shared purpose and aligned activities.

■ **Information Asymmetry**

There is a difference in access to information: One party may have more resources, better connections, or specialized knowledge, giving them an advantage in acquiring relevant information. This lack of availability, accessibility, and transparency can result in an information gap. The black box design creates so much waste.

■ **Fragmented Organization**

A process often involves multiple stakeholders with distinct goals and interests, making the design, business model, and management of their needs challenging for setting up a Lean process.

This asymmetry introduces delays, mistakes, and other wastes in the Voice-of-the-Network system. Addressing the challenges of information asymmetry is essential for a more accurate and collaborative healthcare environment.

Example: Healthcare Process for Maternity Care

To better understand the information asymmetry and fragmented organization, we will describe the care process in four separate steps. Each step acts independently and a "black box" of unknown status makes transactions non-transparent. See Figure 10.3.

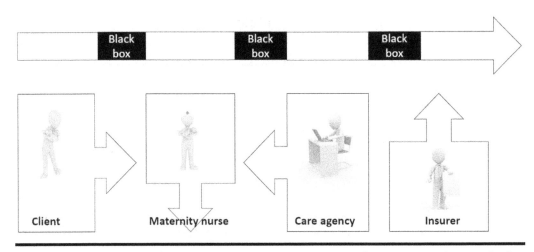

Figure 10.3   Silos in traditional organisations operate as 'Black Boxes' where only the input and outputs are known.

Step 1

The process starts when maternity caregivers manually record their hours on timesheets and let them sign by the patients. Note that the care agency and the insurer are not involved in this process. The care agency and the insurer are only informed at a later moment by pushing information in all kinds of information carriers, paper, email, apps, etc (See Figure 10.4).

Step 2

The maternity care agency processes these records. The client, the maternity nurse, and also the insurer are not involved during this process step. Besides that, most organizations have fragmented departments, roles, functions and authorizations, which contributes to the fragmentation of the entire process (See Figure 10.5).

Step 3

The maternity care agency forwards the data to the insurer via email. The insurer processes this information in its Enterprise Resource Planning system. Note that every organization uses its own systems, taxonomy, abbreviations, and names for processes and products or services. This increases the chance of errors and slows down the turnaround time of the process (See Figure 10.6).

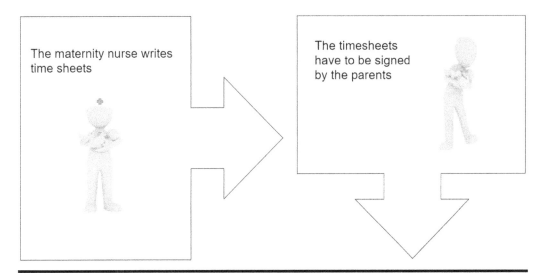

The maternity nurse writes time sheets

The timesheets have to be signed by the parents

Figure 10.4 A 'Push' process in which information and activities are fragmented. Time spent is recorded and approved in separate activities.

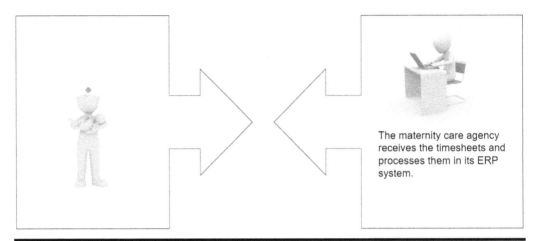

Figure 10.5 A 'Push' process in which information and activities are fragmented. Timesheet processing as a separate activity.

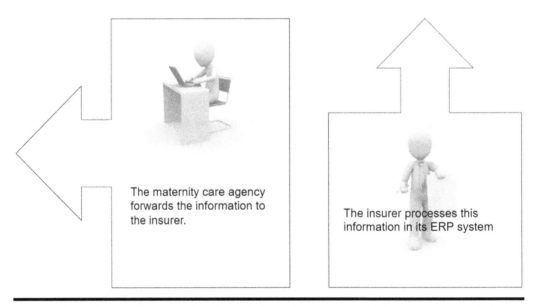

Figure 10.6 A 'Push' process in which information and activities are fragmented. Information flows are inefficient.

Step 4

The synchronization of the entire process takes approximately 90 days. We hope to have made clear that this fragmented administrative procedure is highly inefficient and results in all kinds of operational costs. See Figure 10.7.

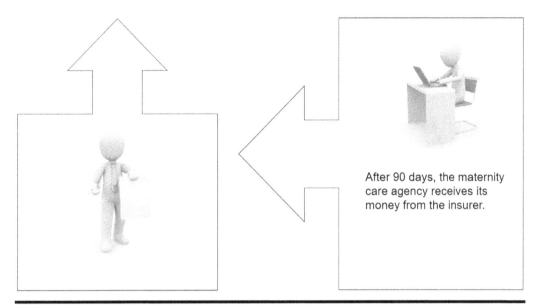

After 90 days, the maternity care agency receives its money from the insurer.

Figure 10.7   A 'Push' process in which information and activities are fragmented. Delays and waiting times are increased.

The problems of information asymmetry in the administrative settlement process is characterized by unnecessary complexity, additional non-value-added tasks and lengthy delays such as 90-day payment delays.

These inefficiencies result in high administrative costs for healthcare institutions, clients, insurers, and society as a whole.

Improve Phase

During our measurement and analysis phases we have discovered that the information asymmetry could be the result of a lack of end-to-end process collaboration, transparency, alignment, motivation, leading to ineffective communications and coordination between stakeholders.

The lack of shared information or instant notification increases errors, variation, inefficiencies, higher costs, and reduces customer satisfaction.

What if we try to improve this inefficient and ineffective process and use a more circular and decentralized organizational design? See Figure 10.8.

Start with System Goals and Purpose

Critical success factors such as safety, quality, reliability, flexibility, costs, and delivery lead time play a crucial role, especially in an environment that depends on aligned and shared information, as previously discussed in

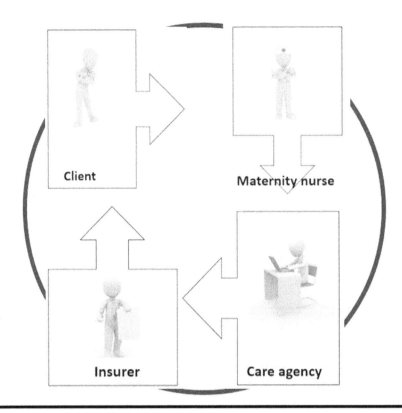

Figure 10.8 A decentralized organizational design using lean systems thinking.

Chapter 4—Cause and Effect. To achieve these objectives, it becomes essential to shift our focus from individual goals to system goals.

To this end, we have developed an innovative ecosystem design framework, a significant change that we will describe in the upcoming Improvement phase.

In addition we introduce the "PIP value-stream model", strategically designed to visualize the value stream and identify bottlenecks arising from insufficient collaboration and poor communications.

In the original Six Sigma philosophy of Motorola and GE, the Improvement phase of DMAIC was focused on implementing a final "solution". However, when this framework is used for Lean Blockchain System Thinking, then the emphasis of the Improve phase shifts **to continuous evolution and improvements reacting to the needs of the system**.

Instead of looking for fixed solutions, the focus is on creating new optimal conditions or **leverage points** based on current knowledge and understanding of the workings of the system. The philosophy prioritizes adaptive improvement and iteration to increase sustainability and flexibility, avoiding the concept of a final or fixed solution.

The Improvement phase is where we can implement many of the transformative possibilities that Blockchain technology offers in addressing and eliminating the root causes that plague TRAD-ORG processes.

The change in thinking from TRAD-ORG to DE-ORG is the key to a more efficient, responsive, and future-proof system. The convergence of Innovative smart technology and proven Lean principles is the key to radical business innovation and improvement.

In the Improvement phase of *Lean Blockchain System Thinking* we move from individual goals to system goals, from centralized control to decentralized consensus, and from hidden information to transparency.

This transition is facilitated by the use of the **Ecosystem Design Framework**[6] with the integration of relationship logic protocol as suggested by Machiel Tesser in 2018. [7]

This model operates on a relationship logic protocol of "if <who> does <what>, then <that>"".

See Figure 10.9.

Who: Identifies the stakeholders/identities involved

What: Identifies their roles and value-adding activities

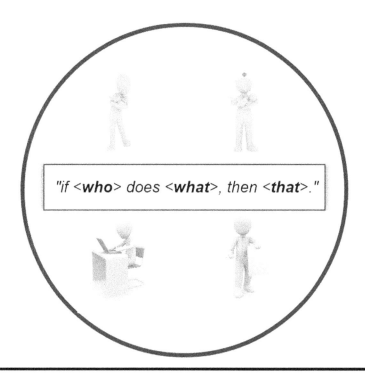

Figure 10.9   The Ecosystem Design Framework6 with the integration of relationship logic protocol as suggested by Machiel Tesser in 2018.

Who + What => That It Happened: The consensus and integration of Who and what information. A proof, a timestamp, a consensus of the fact that something happened with system approval. **That** information is a network status update regarding a predefined system change.

Rules govern this protocol:

> *"if this, then that", IFTTT*

This model provides a structured approach and consensus framework, ensuring clarity and coordination among stakeholders as they collectively work towards systemic goals in a sustainable way.

Control by Design and Intrinsic Value Control Elements

Use of decentralized blockchain frameworks with Systems Thinking leads to a reassessment of which control elements have intrinsic value. Tasks once considered meaningful in centralized systems are losing their meaning within the blockchain framework, especially in the areas of information synchronization, inspection, and third-party validation, governance, and compliance.

Control, Governance, and Compliance based on established rules, guidelines, tolerances, and limits become easier and fairer if all stakeholders are involved in the control phase and have a balanced voice. By preventing a concentration of power within a subset of stakeholders, perverse incentives, conflicting goals, and corruption in the creation of value is avoided.[8]

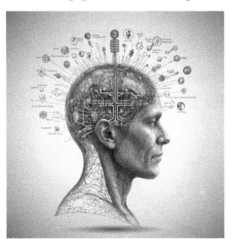

"Long-term value creation can—and should—take into account the interests of all stakeholders".[9]
– Marc Goedhart and Tim Kolle

This framework also facilitates meaningful discussions about impactful and purposeful work, moving away from the traditional pursuit of outcomes that may not meet the client's needs or goals. It focuses on value management and control, through its system design.

Let's highlight some powerful control mechanisms based on Lean principles:

Control and Improve the Flow Mechanism

Decentralization and tokenization promote direct transactions and interactions between participants, bypassing traditional intermediaries. Ensuring consensus and alignment on both the value proposition and the assigned responsibilities is critical for a sustainable system design.

The elimination of waste in these transfer points provides greater control and streamlines operations, reduces costs, and promotes a more efficient, resilient, and transparent ecosystem. See Figure 10.10 for some of the wastes that are eliminated using Lean together with a blockchain toolkit.

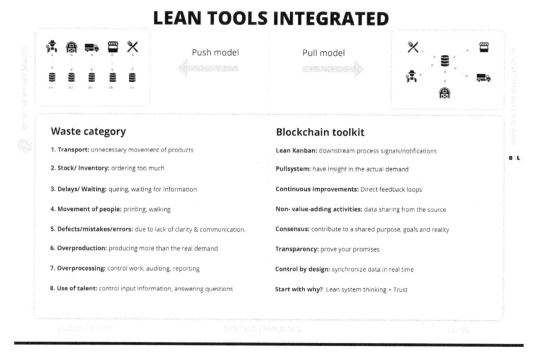

LEAN TOOLS INTEGRATED

Waste category	Blockchain toolkit
1. **Transport:** unnecessary movement of products	**Lean Kanban:** downstream process signals/notifications
2. **Stock/ Inventory:** ordering too much	**Pullsystem:** have insight in the actual demand
3. **Delays/ Waiting:** queing, waiting for information	**Continuous improvements:** Direct feedback loops
4. **Movement of people:** printing, walking	**Non- value-adding activities:** data sharing from the source
5. **Defects/mistakes/errors:** due to lack of clarity & communication.	**Consensus:** contribute to a shared purpose, goals and reality
6. **Overproduction:** producing more than the real demand	**Transparency:** prove your promises
7. **Overprocessing:** control work, auditing, reporting	**Control by design:** synchronize data in real time
8. **Use of talent:** control input information, answering questions	**Start with why?** Lean system thinking + Trust

Figure 10.10   Summary of wastes that are eliminated use Lean together with a blockchain toolkit.

It represents "radical change" better known as a "Lean Kakushin" event, instead of improving the "status Quo" with incremental improvements.

Furthermore, blockchain ensures clarity and data integrity through its secure, transparent, and immutable ledger. Confidence in tamper-proof data eliminates confusion and trust issues associated with centralized or personal data collection and transmission.

Automation is a key feature facilitated by blockchain's decentralized architecture with smart contracts[10] reducing manual tasks and errors. Integration with If-This-Then-That (IFTTT) principles[11] allows initiative-taking detection of undesired results, triggering prompt interventions for non-conforming activities.

Collectively, these advantages of Blockchain technology have a transformative impact on the organizational governance and control landscape. By promoting efficiency, transparency, and automation, Blockchain technology elevated reliability, trust, and security in quality control and management.

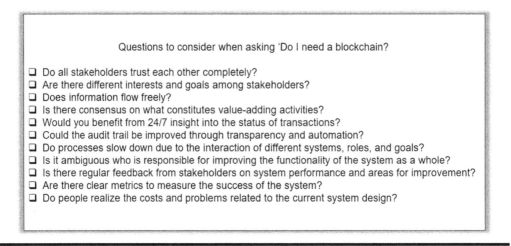

Questions to consider when asking 'Do I need a blockchain?'

❑ Do all stakeholders trust each other completely?
❑ Are there different interests and goals among stakeholders?
❑ Does information flow freely?
❑ Is there consensus on what constitutes value-adding activities?
❑ Would you benefit from 24/7 insight into the status of transactions?
❑ Could the audit trail be improved through transparency and automation?
❑ Do processes slow down due to the interaction of different systems, roles, and goals?
❑ Is it ambiguous who is responsible for improving the functionality of the system as a whole?
❑ Is there regular feedback from stakeholders on system performance and areas for improvement?
❑ Are there clear metrics to measure the success of the system?
❑ Do people realize the costs and problems related to the current system design?

Figure 10.11   Questions to consider when asking 'Do I need a blockchain'.

To highlight the waste caused by our fragmented organizational model, we have listed the waste created per process step in the maternity care process.

This should provide a better understanding of the issues we have come to accept as normal, along with the effects and root causes of this non-collaborative model.

The maternity nurse writes time sheets that they have to sign by the parents.

Non value adding: Printing timesheets, transporting timesheets, stocking timesheets, movement of people, waiting times, etc.

The maternity care agency receives the timesheets and processes them in the ERP system.

Non value adding: Overproduction, overprocessing, waste of talent, waiting times, defects, auditing/controlling information

The maternity care agency forwards the information to the insurer. The insurer processes this information in its ERP system.

Non value adding: Overprocessing; duplicating/synchronizing information in different systems

After 90 days, the maternity care agency receives its money from the insurer.

Non value adding: Waiting for information. Waiting for the payment. Talent underutilized

Figure 10.12   Non value adding activities (wastes) in a traditional organizational structure leading to delays and mistakes.

Lessons

The maternity healthcare scenario illustrates the inefficiencies embedded in our traditional organizational model. A complex administrative settlement process, involving paperwork and a 90-day payment term, reflects the lack of collaboration and poor synchronization within the system. The traditional structure leads to high costs and great dissatisfaction for its stakeholders.

Summary

This chapter emphasizes the need for a methodical and systematic approach to problem-solving and continuous improvement to achieve operational excellence in any organization. In the context of Lean Blockchain, the DMAIC framework is presented as an effective framework to be used in the transition from TRAD-ORG to DE-ORG.

The chapter emphasizes a change in basic assumptions from **individual goals to system goals**, integrating Blockchain technology and Lean principles for radical business innovation.

We have demonstrated the potential and possibilities of DMAIC for identifying and correcting problems within the TRAD-ORG model.

Highlighting the use of Blockchain technology as a solution, we explained how it can enable the 3-flow PIP model and reduce the **information asymmetry and fragmented/siloed organizational structures that are the root causes of much inefficiency in TRAD-ORG models.**

The Improvement phase introduces an innovative *Ecosystem Design Framework* operating with a relationship logic protocol. It provides a structured approach and consensus framework, applying Systems Thinking to a collaborative, environmental, and ecological design.

The Control phase focuses on active monitoring to look for opportunities for further improvements, emphasizing a proactive "control by design" approach. Involving the correct balance of diverse stakeholders at this stage increases the probability of fairer and more sustainable outcomes.

The chapter concludes with questions to help organizations determine whether they need Blockchain technology, considering such aspects as trust, frictionless information flow, consensus, transparency, and procedure automation.

Overall, the chapter demonstrates the potential of DMAIC for identifying and correcting problems in traditional organizational models, TRAD-ORG, and highlights the power of Blockchain technology in the transition to decentralized organizational models, DE-ORG.

Notes

1. Eckes, G. (2000). *The Six Sigma Revolution: How General Electric and Others Turned Process Into Profits.*
2. George, M. L. (2003). **Lean Six Sigma for Service: How to Use Lean Speed and Six Sigma Quality to Improve Services and Transactions.*
3. The concept of 3-flow synchronization in supply chain management involves the coordinated management of product flow, information flow, and payment flow to enhance overall efficiency and performance.
4. The Pareto Principle: A large amount of poor process outcomes are a result of a small amount of defective process inputs. Information asymmetry and fragmented/siloed organizations are the cause of many poor process outcomes in TRAD-ORG structures.
5. See for example: IFTTT. Automate Business & Home. https://en.wikipedia.org/wiki/IFTTT.
6. Hill, S. B. and Rees, G. H. H. (2008). Ecosystem Design and the Challenge of Sustainability. *Ecological Economics*, 67(1), 1–9.
7. Tesser's Ecosystem Design Framework. https://ilssi.org/tessers-ecosystem-design-framework/.
8. Goedhart, M. and Koller, T. (2020). The Value of Value Creation. https://www.mckinsey.com/capabilities/strategy-and-corporate-finance/our-insights/the-value-of-value-creation.
9. Goedhart, M. and Koller, T. (2020, 16 June). McKinsey Quarterly.
10. A "smart contract" is simply a collection of code (its functions) and data (its state) that resides at a specific address on a blockchain. https://ethereum.org/en/developers/docs/smart-contracts/.
11. Oikonomou, L. and Lee, J. C. H. (2010). *IFTTT: Automating the Web with Conditional Logic.* https://ifttt.com.

Index

For Product Safety Concerns and Information please contact our EU
representative GPSR@taylorandfrancis.com
Taylor & Francis Verlag GmbH, Kaufingerstraße 24, 80331 München, Germany